W9-ASK-255

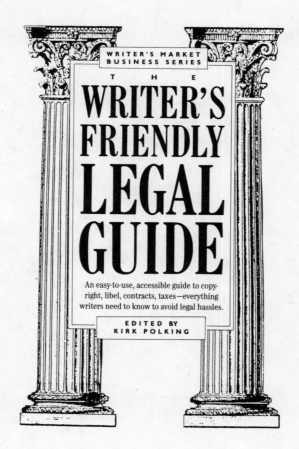

WRITER'S MARKET
BUSINESS SERIES

T H E

WRITER'S FRIENDLY LEGAL GUIDE

An easy-to-use, accessible guide to copyright, libel, contracts, taxes—everything
writers need to know to avoid legal hassles.

EDITED BY
KIRK POLKING

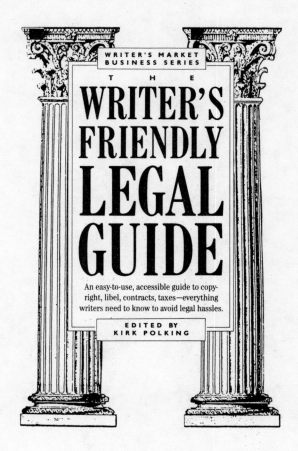

WRITER'S MARKET
BUSINESS SERIES

THE

WRITER'S FRIENDLY LEGAL GUIDE

An easy-to-use, accessible guide to copyright, libel, contracts, taxes—everything
writers need to know to avoid legal hassles.

EDITED BY
KIRK POLKING

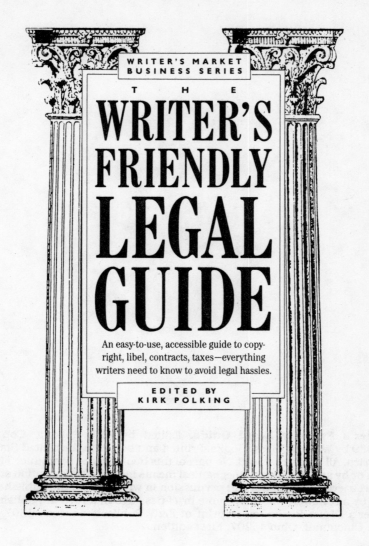

WRITER'S MARKET
BUSINESS SERIES

T H E
WRITER'S FRIENDLY LEGAL GUIDE

An easy-to-use, accessible guide to copyright, libel, contracts, taxes—everything writers need to know to avoid legal hassles.

EDITED BY
KIRK POLKING

'ennessee Tech. Library
Cookeville, Tenn.

Writer's
Digest
Books

Cincinnati, Ohio

Writer's Friendly Legal Guide. Edited by Kirk Polking. Copyright
© 1989 by Writer's Digest Books. Printed and bound in the United States of
America. All rights reserved. No part of this book may be reproduced in any
form or by an electronic or mechanical means including information storage
and retrieval systems without permission in writing from the publisher, except by a reviewer, who may quote brief passages in a review. Published by
Writer's Digest Books, an imprint of F&W Publications, Inc., 1507 Dana
Ave., Cincinnati, Ohio 45207. First edition.

Library of Congress Cataloging-in-Publication Data

Writer's friendly legal guide / edited by Kirk Polking.
    p. cm.
  Rev. ed. of: Law and the writer / edited by Kirk Polking and
Leonard S. Meranus. 3rd ed. c1985.
    Bibliography: p.
    Includes index.
    ISBN 0-89879-373-4
  1. Authors and publishers—United States. 2. Copyright—United
States. I. Polking, Kirk. II. Law and the writer.
KF3084.W75   1989
346.7304'82—dc20
[347.306482]   89-33031
                                  CIP

Table of Contents

Preface...x

Quick Information Finder...xii

1. The Freelance Writer and Freedom of the Press...1
William E. Francois

2. Invasion of Privacy...13
Harry M. Johnston III and Laury M. Frieber

3. Avoiding Libel Suits...23
Michael S. Lasky

4. Fiction Can Be Dangerous, Too!...35
Carol E. Rinzler

5. Pornography and the Serious Writer...43
Herald Price Fahringer

6. Photography and the Law...47
Richard H. Logan III

7. Ten Questions About Copyright...59
Victor W. Marton

8. Protecting Your Ideas in Hollywood...73
Lionel S. Sobel

9. Your First Book Contract...85
Georges Borchardt

10. Trends in Subsidiary Rights...95
Perry H. Knowlton

11. Other Writing Contracts...103

12. Syndication Contracts...109
Richard S. Newcombe

13. Federal Taxes and the Writer...113
Patricia Fox Fleck

14. Social Security and the Self-Employed Writer...121
Louise Boggess

15. The Author's Estate...139
Arthur F. Abelman

About the Authors...147

Glossary of Legal Terms...151

Bibliography...165

Index...169

Preface

"The glorious uncertainty" is how one writer defined the law, and if there is one certainty, it is that the law will change. *The Writer's Friendly Legal Guide* reflects those changes. For example, a sustained effort by writers and artists to get an amendment to the 1986 Tax Reform Act passed by Congress paid off in October 1988 and is detailed in Chapter Thirteen in this book. The original act brought cries of outrage from writers and artists who had to withhold deducting their expenses until they could apportion each ream of paper and tube of paint to a specific published or paid for bit of creative work. The Act has now been revised to allow deductions to be taken as they are incurred. The caveat remains, however, that you must make a profit in three out of five years for your writing to be considered a business, not a hobby. There are other changes worth noting, too:

In March 1989, the United States joined the worldwide Berne Copyright Convention so those changes affecting writers are included in our chapter on Copyright (Chapter Seven).

The Writers Guild strike of 1988 brought changes in the rates producers pay screenwriters for film and teleplay scripts, and you'll find those in the charts in Chapter Eleven.

Changing author relationships with book publishers reflected in the advances now being paid and the percentages offered for subsidiary rights are detailed in Chapters Nine and Ten.

New Format. As the title of this book implies, we have made the updated information from previous editions of this book (formerly *Law and the Writer*) more accessible to the reader in several ways: (1) A page and type design that permits you to quickly see the salient points of each chapter; (2) A brief introduction to each chapter that highlights the contents and a summary review at the end; (3) A preview of the more detailed General Index—a Quick Information Finder —which zeroes in on the points you'll most likely want to refer to.

The Writer's Friendly Legal Guide is designed to present an introduction to major areas of concern—freedom of speech, libel, privacy, copyright—and to alert the writer to laws and regulations affecting his "business" of writing. The Bibliography shows where to look further.

Finding a Lawyer. There is no substitute for a lawyer when a writer has legal problems. The writer, though, can avoid most legal difficulties by being aware of troublesome areas and having a general understanding of the laws relating to them. That is the purpose of this book.

Although the Supreme Court's ruling now permits lawyers to advertise, it is still not an easy task to find a lawyer with specific detailed experience in literary or publishing law. As you might expect, the majority are located in publishing centers like New York, but two directories you might want to consult in your nearest large public or college library are the *Martindale-Hubbell Law Directory* and the *Directory of Intellectual Property Lawyers and Patent Agents*.

How Much Do Lawyers Charge? What kind of fees can a writer expect to pay an attorney? The answer depends on a number of factors such as prevailing rates in the community, the type of legal problem, the degree of expertise required, and in some cases, the result. Although there are significant exceptions, most lawyers charge hourly rates. Depending on the nature of the legal matter, hourly rates could range from $50 to $75 an hour for a lawyer in a rural community or a young lawyer in a law firm, and up to $200 an hour or more for a senior partner in a law firm in a major city. In some situations, such as plaintiffs' lawsuits, lawyers will take cases on a contingent fee basis, with the fee based on the amount recovered. Again, depending on the type of case and whether it is settled, goes to trial, or is appealed, contingent fees are usually in the range of 25 to 40 percent of the amount recovered. Court costs and other out-of-pocket expenses are customarily paid from the award. If there is no recovery, the lawyer gets no fee, but the client is still responsible for expenses.

When retaining a lawyer, it is advisable to discuss fees with him in advance. Lawyers are accustomed to such inquiries and usually keep written records of their time so they can substantiate their charges.

Your Comments Are Welcome. Future editions of this book will reflect changes in the law as they occur. In addition, we invite freelance writers to tell us about personal experiences touching on any of the chapters so that we can, where possible, share them (without using your name) with other writers through future editions of *The Writer's Friendly Legal Guide*.

Kirk Polking

Quick Information Finder

The information in this volume is essential to the writer in today's litigious society. Learning in advance about possible pitfalls can help you avoid problems and anxieties over your manuscripts.

In this Quick Information Finder, we have picked some of the topics of most interest to writers and listed where they may be found throughout the book. This list isn't trying to compete with the complete index found on page 169, it's just here to help you find major topics quickly and to pique your interest in this vital subject.

Access to Private Documents...14–15
Accurate Reporting Versus Truth...25–26
"Actual Malice" and Libel...2–5, 18, 19, 26–28, 32–33, 40
Average Advances: Fiction & Nonfiction...86–87
Book Clubs...88, 98–99
Broadcasting...9, 64–65, 103–107
Child Pornography...45–46
Commercial Rights...99–100
Copyright in Collective Works...62–63
Copyright Notice...52, 61
Copyright on Photos...51–52
Copyright Term and Renewal...63
Deductible Expenses...116–117
Depreciation Schedules...115–118
Disability Claims...129–133
Disclaimers in Fiction...37
Disclosing Subject's Distant Past...21–22
Disguising Characters from Life...37–39
Fair Trial...8, 55
Fair Use...63–65
Fictionalizing in True Stories...18–19, 35–36, 37–38, 40
Fiction and Public Figures...40–41
Foreign Rights...88, 89, 99–100
Freedom of Information Act...7–8
Home Office Deduction...113–114
Insurance...29–30, 52–54, 90
Limits on Student Press...10
Medicare...132–133
Misappropriation of Name or Likeness...5, 15, 17, 47
Model Releases...47–48
Movie Rights...88, 97–98
Net Versus List Royalties...86–87
Obscenity Standards...8–9, 43–45, 50–51

Option Clause...90–91
Ownership Clause...111
Paperback Rights...87–88, 89–90, 96–97
Photos and Libel...30–31, 50
Photographic Ethics...55–56
Protecting Ideas...61, 74–80
Protecting Sources...5–7, 26
Public Interest...4–5, 26
Publishing from the Public Record...7–8, 20–21
Qualifying for Social Security...121–125
Reconstructing Dialogue...19
Registering Copyright...61
Retirement Earnings...128–129
Royalties for Playwrights...103
Self-Employment Tax Rates...125
Serial Rights...88–97
Shield Laws...5–7, 26
Survivor's Insurance...134–135
Syndication Contracts...109–111
Taping Telephone Calls...15
Three Elements of Libel...24
TV and Film Rate Schedules...103–107
Warranty Clause...90
Writers Guild Registration...81–82

Chapter 1
The Freelance Writer and Freedom of the Press

William E. Francois

For the most part, freelance writers enjoy the same rights and privileges accorded full-time journalists—but there are some exceptions. This chapter will outline:

1. Two areas where the law treats freelancers and full-time journalists equally: when the courts try to stop publication of an article and when law enforcement officers want to search a writer's office.

2. The critical factors in determining whether a story is libelous or invades another's privacy, and how those factors apply to a freelancer.

3. Why freelancers are at a definite disadvantage when seeking to protect their sources.

4. Where freelancers stand when seeking access to official government documents.

5. Guidelines for freelancers on fair trial issues, obscenity laws, and television or radio reporting.

Do freelance writers enjoy the same protection of the law as full-time journalists? The answer depends on which kind of law is being examined. There are these kinds of law: constitutional, common law, case law, statutory law, and regulatory law (the latter resulting from rules and regulations put forth by various regulatory agencies, such as the Federal Communications Commission and Federal Trade Commission). In addition, laws can be subdivided into federal law, state law, and the laws of smaller political entities, such as cities, counties, school districts, etc. If we look at constitutional law, and specifically the protection afforded freelance writers by the First Amendment, generally what we find is that the First Amendment does not make a distinction between freelancers and "professional journalists." They are equally protected or equally vulnerable, depending on one's point of view.

One example of vulnerability is the situation of freelance writer

Howard Morland who wrote an article for *The Progressive* magazine entitled "The H-Bomb Secret—How We Got It, Why We're Telling It." The magazine was enjoined from publishing the article by U.S. District Court Judge Robert Warren in Madison, Wisconsin, and the magazine appealed. Before the appeal could be decided, another Madison publication, the *Press Connection*, published a letter from a computer programmer that explained how the H-bomb worked. The Justice Department then dropped its case for the injunction.

Central to the First Amendment is the idea that *most* prior restraints of the press are unconstitutional. But the door has been left ajar by past decisions of the U.S. Supreme Court for the imposition of such restraints under certain circumstances.

Judge Warren believed that publication of the article—even though some of the major facts in it were available to the public—contained interpretive information that, when synthesized with the information since reclassified as secret, would violate secrecy provisions of the Atomic Energy Act and would likely cause "direct, immediate, and irreparable injury" to the nation. The point is, the outcome of this case does not hinge on whether the writer of the article was a freelancer or a staff writer.

Similarly, freelance writers are not protected by the First Amendment, any more than are "professional" journalists and their organizations, against an unannounced search of an "innocent party's" office or home by law enforcement officers armed with a search warrant. That was the gist of the U.S. Supreme Court's five-to-three decision in 1978 (*Zurcher v. Stanford Daily*) following a search of the student newspaper's office at Stanford University. Police were searching for photographs that might have been used to identify demonstrators who injured several police officers.

It should be emphasized that the decision in no way weakens the Fourth Amendment's bar against *unreasonable* search and seizure.

As a consequence of the *Zurcher* decision, the Carter Administration proposed legislation in 1979 that was subsequently passed. It greatly restricts searches of homes and offices of persons not suspected of crimes. The legislation not only protects the press, but specifically includes freelance writers and photographers. Several states also have taken steps to offset the potential effect of the *Zurcher* decision.

Freelancers and Libel

Concerning the protectiveness of the First Amendment, the critical factor is not *who*—staff writer or freelancer—wrote or said something, but rather *what* was said or printed about *whom*. For example, in 1964, in the case of *New York Times v. Sullivan*, the U.S. Supreme Court unanimously expanded the protection afforded by the First Amendment in order to reduce the likelihood of success-ful libel actions brought by *public officials* against the news media. Even when probably false statements were published about such offi-cials, a successful suit for damages was no longer inevitable. The Court voted to protect *some* false statements in order to make public debate more robust and uninhibited, and to reduce the threat of large damage awards in libel actions that were having a chilling effect on First Amendment freedoms.

Proving "Actual Malice"

The new First Amendment standard requires that such officials must show "actual malice" on the part of publisher or writer before a lawsuit can succeed, and "actual malice" is defined as knowingly publishing falsehoods, or reckless disregard of the truth. Significantly, it makes no difference who writes the libelous story. If the public official can prove actual malice by "clear and convincing evidence," he or she can win a lawsuit against the publisher and writer.

The Supreme Court also extended the "actual malice" rule to in-clude defamation lawsuits by *public figures.* The extent of such pro-tection is illustrated by an 8-0 decision of the Supreme Court in *Hustler Magazine v. Falwell.* A jury had reached a finding of inten-tional or reckless misconduct on the part of Larry Flynt's *Hustler Magazine* in publishing a parody advertisement aimed at the Rev. Jerry Falwell. The advertisement was intended to parody an advertis-ing campaign for a liqueur with Falwell purportedly being interviewed and revealing an incestuous relationship with his mother. At the bottom of the full-page ad was this disclaimer: "Ad Parody—Not to Be Taken Seriously." And it was listed in the table of contents as "Fiction: Ad and Personality Parody."

The trial court dismissed Falwell's invasion of privacy action, and the jury ruled against Falwell on his libel claim. But on the minis-ter's emotional distress allegation, the jury awarded Falwell $100,000 in actual damages and $50,000 in punitive damages against pub-lisher Flynt, and $50,000 in punitive damages from the magazine.

When the case reached the Supreme Court in 1988, the justices reversed the jury award, saying that a public figure (or public official) who seeks to recover damages for intentional infliction of emotional distress must demonstrate that the publication contained false state-ment of fact made with *actual malice.* As Chief Justice William H. Rehnquist pointed out in his opinion for the Court, the ad in ques-tion—though gross and repugnant to most people—could not reason-ably have been interpreted as stating actual facts about the public figure involved.

The Court's application of the *New York Times-Sullivan* standard to the question posed by the *Hustler-Falwell* case demonstrates anew the conviction of the Supreme Court that adequate "breathing space" must be allowed for the freedoms guaranteed by the First Amendment.

In connection with proving "actual malice," the U.S. Supreme Court ruled, in a 6–3 decision in *Herbert v. Lando* in April 1979 that under certain circumstances libel plaintiffs could inquire into the state of mind of journalists or writers, or into the editorial process, when such inquiry is of critical importance to the plaintiff's lawsuit. This decision was widely denounced by the press as a blow to First Amendment values. But the majority of justices in *Herbert* declared that "relevant" questioning of a potential libel defendant by the plaintiff's attorney constitutes one of the ways in which such a plaintiff can meet the heavy burden of showing "actual malice." The Court thus rejected a constitutional privilege against such inquiries despite the press's assertion that such inquiries would pose a threat to First Amendment freedoms.

Although the First Amendment "actual malice" rule now includes public officials and public figures, it does not extend to private individuals except in jury determinations of punitive damage awards. A private individual—generally defined by the U.S. Supreme Court as a person who has not voluntarily thrust himself or herself into the public limelight or achieved pervasive fame or notoriety—must, in most states, show actual malice in order to recover punitive, or exemplary, damages.

Problems of definition exist. It's not always easy to distinguish between a public figure and a private individual, and yet First Amendment protection hinges, in part, on the type of individual who's been libeled in a story.

In most states, a private individual can recover *general* and/or *special* damages for libelous reports by showing that such statements, resulting from negligence on the part of the media defendant, caused *actual injury* (such as damage to good name, loss of business, etc.).

The Newsworthiness Factor

There is another factor to be considered: namely, the "nature" of the story. Generally, First Amendment protection will be accorded to stories or articles that are of *public interest*, or *in* the public interest, or *newsworthy*. Some courts, especially those in California and in Florida, have added a qualifier—*legitimate* public interest—to denote the kind of published information that is constitutionally protected in the sense that actual malice must be shown before a lawsuit can be successful. The distinction is between mere public curiosity and information of genuine public concern. Again, definitions are a problem. Not all judges would define the content of a given story or article as being of public interest, or newsworthy. And where the content is not so defined, considerable First Amendment protection is lost.

For example, if you write a story about alleged corruption in your city or county government, or you examine the care afforded to the elderly, such a story undoubtedly would be considered newsworthy or in the public interest. Articles about *recent* crimes and the perpetrators of those crimes fall into the public interest-newsworthy category. But what about articles that resurrect the past, particularly those that identify the people who committed the crimes that happened long ago? Might not the state have an interest in the rehabilitation of such persons who, by now, may be living useful, productive lives in society? California and Florida courts have considered such circumstances in deciding whether a magazine article is or is not newsworthy and therefore entitled to the protection of the First Amendment.

Invasion of Privacy

The newsworthiness test is also a defense against some invasion of privacy lawsuits. If an article is newsworthy, if it is not published with actual malice, and if it does not disclose any private facts which might be offensive to a reasonable person, then in all likelihood the First Amendment protects such publication. Generally speaking, the news media are accorded considerable latitude in deciding what is and what is not newsworthy; but the ultimate decision, should a libel or invasion of privacy lawsuit result, rests with the courts.

At this point I should emphasize a cardinal rule; namely, the First Amendment is not a license to trespass, steal, or intrude by electronic or other means into the privacy of another person's home or office. Nor does the First Amendment give the media the right to use a person's name or likeness for commercial purposes without first obtaining that person's approval. Therefore, don't rely on the First Amendment to protect you from an invasion of privacy suit if you use a person's photograph in an advertisement without first obtaining that person's consent, or if you open another person's mail to obtain information, or eavesdrop on a telephone conversation. Under such circumstances, the First Amendment won't ward off lawsuits.

Freelancers May Not Be Able to Shield Sources

Turning to state laws, there is one type of statute that generally does not accord freelancers the protection given to "professional journalists." About half of the states statutorily provide that under certain conditions journalists do not have to disclose confidential sources. In most of these states the term *journalist* does not include a freelance writer. For example, New York's "shield" law originally stated that "no professional journalist . . . shall be adjudged in contempt of any court" for refusing to disclose the source of any news coming into his possession. In early 1979 a New York court held that the law, Section 79-h of the Civil Rights Law, does not protect a book author from having to produce notes and tape recordings in connection with an interview of a prosecution witness in a murder trial. Several months later the Appellate Division of the New York Supreme Court upheld the lower court's interpretation of the "shield law," saying that a book author's interest in protecting confidential information is "less compelling than that of a journalist or newsman." The law later was amended to protect freelance journalists. Arizona's law provides that "any person employed by the news media" may shield confidential sources of news. Most of the state laws allow "professional news persons" to shield confidential sources. In California, prior to 1975, the courts interpreted the much-amended shield law as protecting newspaper and radio-TV journalists, but not magazine journalists. The law was amended in 1975 to remedy this. Freelancers should let their legislators know that those who write magazine articles and books warrant equal protection whenever shield legislation is being considered.

Very few of the state shield laws provide "absolute" protection; and in some there are so many loopholes that the journalist is virtually unprotected. In fact, the New Mexico Supreme Court struck down the shield law in that state in 1976 because the court believed the law infringed upon the judiciary's function. The law, in the opinion of the court, infringed upon the separation of powers doctrine because the legislature was attempting to tell the courts what they could or could not do by way of compelling witnesses—journalists—to disclose certain information on pain of contempt of court. A similar result was recorded in California courts but the voters in that state then amended the state constitution to provide absolute protection against forced disclosure.

Federal Shield Law Possible

For a time in the late 1960s and early 1970s, journalists contended that the First Amendment gave them a right to shield confidential sources; but in 1972 the U.S. Supreme Court *seemed* to say that reporters cannot refuse to answer questions put to them by properly constituted investigative bodies, such as grand juries, when criminal matters are being probed. *Seemed* to say this because the Court split five to four and one of the associate justices, Lewis F. Powell Jr., wrote what has been described as an "enigmatic" concurring opinion, thereby leaving considerable uncertainty about the right of journalists to refuse to disclose confidential sources under the First Amendment guarantee of free speech. One of the reasons cited by the majority of the Court in apparently deciding against such right was the difficulty of determining who would qualify for the protection. Would anyone who writes for the media have the constitutional right to refuse to answer questions put to them by a lawfully constituted investigative body? Freelancers? "Underground" journalists?

The Supreme Court observed that Congress could, if it wished, pass a federal shield law and decide the issue statutorily. Congress has not yet chosen to legislate in this area even though many bills have been introduced since the 1972 decision by the Supreme Court. One of the things you can do is write your representative in Congress urging the inclusion of freelancers in the "reach" of such protective legislation.

Interestingly, freelancers did gain a measure of protection from being subpoenaed to testify before grand juries when the Justice Department amended its guidelines in late 1975. Under guidelines that were issued in 1970, only full-time staffers of the "establishment" news media probably were protected from harassment by federal attorneys by the requirement that such officials obtain the personal approval of the U.S. attorney general before a subpoena could be issued. Additionally, all other potential sources for the information being sought first had to be exhausted before the newsperson could be summoned to appear before a federal grand jury. But in 1975, the then United States attorney general, Edward Levi, expanded the protection of the guidelines to include anyone "engaged in reporting public affairs." This broadened the Justice Department's regulations to include authors, documentary film producers, and representatives of the nontraditional press. Freelancers clearly are included within these guidelines.

Seeking Government Documents

Concerning the collection of information, as contrasted with attempts to shield information or the sources of information, freelancers are on an equal footing with other information-seekers who wish to use the Freedom of Information Act (FOIA) to compel the federal government to disclose.

FOIA went into effect July 4, 1967, providing the public with its first legal right to know what the federal government is doing. Some important changes were made in the law in 1974 to facilitate the flow of information to the public, although there remain nine categories of information that are exempt from disclosure. These categories are national security-foreign affairs, internal practices of an agency, interagency memoranda, investigatory files, trade or commercial secrets, personnel and medical files, reports on regulation of financial institutions, geological data, and data specifically exempt from disclosure under other laws.

The Federal Bureau of Investigation and the Central Intelligence Agency were inundated with FOIA requests in 1976 and 1977 and had to make special staff arrangements to handle them. Records show that the most frequently used exemptions to disclosure were the investigatory files and interagency memoranda categories. And the turndowns sparked considerable litigation. FOIA allows a lawsuit to be filed in U.S. District Courts in an effort to force disclosure, and the courts are given the authority to inspect records *in camera* (privately) to determine if any or all of the information has been wrongfully withheld by the agency.

A freelancer who wishes to use FOIA to pry information from a federal agency must reasonably describe the records or information being sought. The request should be sent to the appropriate agency which has ten working days in which to decide whether to comply with the request. Several agencies, including the FBI and the CIA, were granted an extension of time to comply with FOIA requests because of the heavy backlog. In those instances, courts ordered the requests to be handled on a first-in, first-out basis.

Freelancers' quest for information received additional support from a series of U.S. Supreme Court decisions in 1975 and 1976. The Court, in substance, held that the judiciary or a state could not prevent the media from publishing truthful, accurate information that is a part of public judicial records. In other words, what is on the public court record can be published, notwithstanding a law or judge's order to the contrary. Thus, a freelancer sitting in open court cannot be constitutionally denied the right to publish whatever is on the record of that court.

Free Press vs. Fair Trial

The cases which led to such a declaration involved the identification of a rape victim, contrary to Georgia state law; a judge's order in Nebraska prohibiting publication of certain information in connection with a murder trial, such as the existence of a confession; and a judge's order prohibiting the press from identifying an Oklahoma youth who had been charged in connection with a slaying. In the three cases, the information that was ordered withheld or forbidden by law from being published already had been disclosed in the public records of judicial proceedings.

The conflict between press and judiciary stems from occasional clashes between the First Amendment guarantee of free speech and the Sixth Amendment, which requires a "speedy and public trial, by an impartial jury." Sometimes legislatures and courts, in their efforts to ensure an impartial jury, enact laws or issue orders that are overly protective and result in prior restraint of the press. As a general rule, such restraint is unconstitutional.

Obscenity Hard to Define

Another area of the law that occasionally may be troublesome to writers and/or photographers pertains to obscenity. To begin with, the definitional problem is enormous. The Supreme Court has been struggling for decades to come up with a definition that is tolerable in the light of the First Amendment. Once something has been legally defined as obscene, it no longer is protected by the First Amendment. In 1973 a majority of the U.S. Supreme Court changed the test of what constitutes obscenity. The three-part test laid down in *Miller v. California* is: (1) whether the average person, applying contemporary community standards, would find that the work, taken as a whole, appeals to prurient interest; (2) whether the work depicts or describes, in a patently offensive way, sexual conduct specifically defined by the applicable state law; and (3) whether the work, taken as a whole, lacks serious literary, artistic, political, or scientific value.

In regard to the third prong, the Supreme Court, in a divided 5–4 opinion in 1987, said that the test for determining whether the allegedly obscene material "lacks serious literary, artistic, political, or scientific value" is "whether a reasonable person would find such value in the material, taken as a whole."

There has been considerable debate and various legal results, and the Supreme Court is itself split, usually by a six-to-three or five-to-four margin, as to how specific the applicable state or federal law must be. Also, there's a troublesome question: Who decides what the contemporary community standards are? A majority of the Supreme Court currently holds that local community juries do this, but therein lies a problem. Concededly, what is obscene can vary from community to community. Nonetheless, many convictions on obscenity grounds are being upheld by the United States Supreme Court. And yet the author of several Supreme Court decisions that enunciated obscenity standards prior to the *Miller* case, William Brennan Jr., had this to say in a dissenting opinion in *Miller*:

" . . . [A]fter 15 years of experimentation and debate I am reluctantly forced to the conclusion that none of the available formulas, including the one announced today, can reduce the vagueness to a tolerable level while at the same time striking an acceptable balance between the protections of the First and Fourteenth Amendments, on the one hand, and on the other the asserted state interest in regulating the dissemination of certain sexually oriented materials." (See Chapter Five for more on this issue.)

Different Rules for Different Media?

There are other, equally troubling, legal questions pertaining to the rights enshrined in the First Amendment. For example, can the First Amendment be differently applied to the mass media? The answer is yes. Radio and TV are more regulatable than is the print medium. There are reasons given for this, including the arguments that the public owns the airwaves, licensees are fiduciaries or proxies for the public, and, according to several decisions, TV is the most powerful medium of mass communication and therefore is subject to more governmental regulation.

Limits on Student Press

A parallel question can be raised vis-a-vis the student press and First Amendment guarantees. Do student journalists enjoy the same protection as the "pros"? The Supreme Court said in 1969, in *Tinker v. Des Moines Independent School District*, that students are possessed of fundamental rights which the state must respect. Among these is freedom of expression.

But the Court, in a 5–3 decision in *Hazelwood School District v. Kuhlmeier* (1988), ruled that a public high school student newspaper that was produced by the school's journalism class and was not open to "indiscriminate use" by student reporters or editors or by the student body generally, is not a public forum. Therefore, the First Amendment is not violated by school officials, who exercise editorial control over the style and content of student speech in such school-sponsored expressive activities, if such action is reasonably related to legitimate pedagogical concerns.

This case arose after the school principal deleted two pages of a newspaper issue that included an article describing students' experiences with pregnancy and another one that discussed the impact of divorce on students at the school. The divorce article contained the name of a student who complained about her father's conduct, and the principal feared that the students interviewed for the pregnancy article might be identified even though their names were not used.

Justice Byron R. White gave the opinion for the Court, noting that the First Amendment rights of *public* school students are not automatically coextensive with the rights of adults. Such a school need not tolerate student speech that is inconsistent with its "basic educational mission," said White.

In reading this case, special attention should be drawn to the following: (1) the ruling applies only to public schools—not to private ones where government usually is not involved and therefore the requisite "government action" threatening basic freedoms is not at issue; (2) the newspaper was the product of a journalism class—a "laboratory" newspaper, so to speak, and not a public forum or an extracurricular activity by and for all kinds of students with the newspaper "open" to stories, etc., from a variety of sources and/or staffers; and (3) the principal was deemed by the Court to have acted "reasonably" in this situation. In this or comparable situations, public school students do not enjoy the same First Amendment rights as adults.

As the record shows, neither do freelance journalists or writers enjoy in all instances the same protection or "rights" as professional journalists do. Where inequalities exist in the law, freelancers can agitate to redress such disparities. They have met with some successes in the past and will continue to do so in the future.

Review/Chapter 1

Constitutional law applies equally to freelance writers and full-time journalists in these areas:

✔prior restraint
✔unannounced searches by law enforcement
✔libel
✔invasion of privacy
✔Freedom of Information Act inquiries

Whether freelance writers can be held in contempt of court for refusing to reveal their sources depends on:

✔the laws of the state in which they live or work

Factors that help determine whether a libel lawsuit can succeed include:

✔whether the person in question is a public or private figure
✔whether the story is in the public interest

The Freedom of Information Act allows government officials to withhold nine types of documents. The types most frequently withheld are:

✔interagency memoranda
✔investigatory files

The U.S. Supreme Court ruled in 1988 that student journalists do not always enjoy the same First Amendment rights as adult journalists. The Court said editorial control by school officials is acceptable when:

✔the school is a public school
✔the newspaper is not a public forum for all kinds of students, but rather is a product of a class
✔the editorial control is reasonably related to legitimate educational concerns

Chapter 2
Invasion of Privacy

Harry M. Johnston III and Laury M. Frieber

Everyone has the right to be left alone. As a writer, you need to know how to distinguish between the public's right to know and your subject's right to privacy. This chapter will help you understand privacy issues, which include:

1. Whether you could be held liable for using false pretenses to gain information, accepting materials you know were obtained illegally, or taping telephone calls without the other party's consent.

2. Whether you have to get a person's permission to use his or her name or picture in a publication.

3. When fictionalizing elements in a basically true story (such as reconstructing dialogue) is okay and when it may be an invasion of privacy.

4. Whether you could be held liable if you use true but embarrassing information about someone, such as a criminal record in a person's distant past or the name of a rape victim.

The specter of the systematic accumulation of vast amounts of personal data about individuals by public and private agencies of all kinds has generated much fresh interest in the citizen's right of privacy. As this and other new facets of the right of privacy develop, it is important to realize that publishers and writers have long been subject to liability for invasion of several different rights of privacy. The publication in 1890 of an immensely influential article by Louis Brandeis and Samuel Warren articulated the notion that it was necessary to protect an individual against a press perceived by the authors as "overstepping in every direction the obvious bounds of propriety and decency." Against such a press, Brandeis and Warren argued, the individual had a right of privacy.

What Is "Right of Privacy"?

The right of privacy has been described as "the right to be let alone; to live one's life as one chooses, free from assault, intrusion, or invasion except as they can be justified by the clear needs of community living under a government of law." The term "right of privacy" is a general one, and there are included under it many particular privacy rights enjoyed by individuals in our society. Of these many particular rights, there are four that are of particular interest to writers and publishers. Specifically, an individual may find protection against:

1. Intrusion
2. Misappropriation of his or her name
3. Publicity that places the person in a false light before the public
4. Publicity that discloses private and embarrassing facts

What follows is a brief exploration of each of these areas of potential liability for writers and publishers.

Intrusion

Perhaps the least complex of the four notions of privacy, this theory says that living individuals are protected against the acquisition of information from or about them which is accomplished through intrusion, i.e., "intrusion whether by physical trespass or not, into spheres from which an ordinary man . . . could reasonably expect that the [reporter] should be excluded."

Using False Pretenses to Gather News

Intrusion claims arise in a number of contexts in which individuals employ subterfuge to gather information, obtain access to private property, or eavesdrop. The legal rules vary from state to state as to whether the use of subterfuge or "false pretenses" to obtain information is actionable, but a claim for invasion of privacy may be successful where false pretenses are employed to gain access to someone's private premises. Thus, in a leading case, the surreptitious photographing and radio recording of an alleged medical quack by individuals (including a reporter) posing as patients to gain admittance to his home/office was found to be an invasion of privacy. The fact that these actions had been undertaken to gather news did not serve as a defense.

In general, writers and reporters who wish to enter private premises (such as an individual's home, office, hospital room, etc.) to gather information should obtain permission to do so from an individual who reasonably appears to have authority to give such permission. Where story subjects are located in an institution such as a hospital or school, it may be necessary to obtain permission from the administrator in charge of the institution as well as from the story subject who occupies the hospital room or classroom. Keep in mind that there is no First Amendment privilege to trespass on private property for purposes of newsgathering. Moreover, consent may well not be a successful defense to an intrusion claim if the reporter exceeded the scope of the consent that was given.

As a general rule, a writer will not be liable for invasion of privacy by obtaining access to private documents, so long as he or she does not participate in, encourage, or suggest any unlawful acts to obtain the property but is merely a passive recipient of them. This rule holds even if the writer knows the material is stolen. In one case, a columnist was held not liable for intrusion for disclosing the contents of a senator's private papers that had been stolen from the senator's office by one of his staffers who provided them to the columnist.

Taping Telephone Calls

Wiretapping and electronic eavesdropping have also been alleged to be intrusive invasions of privacy and are prohibited under a federal criminal statute. The federal statute does not, however, prohibit taping of telephone conversations by a party to the conversation, so long as the recording is not done for an illegal purpose. The federal law governs only interstate conversations; telephone conversations that take place entirely within a single state (as opposed to interstate) may be subject to state laws that prohibit taping even with one party's participation. Many states do require the consent of both parties before taping can be undertaken and so the writer interested in taping with one-party consent only will have to clarify the law of the state in which the taping will take place. (As a protection in any case, most freelancers ask their interviewees when the telephone conversation begins if they may record [for factual accuracy] and if the subject agrees, they then proceed and the subject's advance agreement on the tape is their backup.)

Misappropriation

Most states—either by common law or by statute—recognize a cause of action arising from the commercial use of a person's name or likeness without the person's consent (which can sometimes, of course, be secured only by payment). Several states have a statute modeled after that of New York, which reads in part as follows: "Any person whose name, portrait, or picture is used within this state for advertising purposes or for the purposes of trade without the written consent first obtained . . . may maintain an equitable action . . . against the person, firm or corporation so using his name, portrait, or picture, to prevent and restrain the use thereof; and may also sue and recover damages for any injuries sustained by reason of such use . . . " New York rules are not binding in other states, but the general acceptance of the principles they embody makes consideration of them appropriate.

The News Exception

Read literally, New York's statute would appear to prevent a daily newspaper from recounting the previous night's events at, say, a po-

litical rally—and from depicting these events through published photographs—without acquiring the prior written consent of every
individual whose name or face appeared in the report. Of course,
such consents are unnecessary and the political rally example illus-
trates the *news* exception to the requirements of the statute. Thus,
even though it has been contended that the newspaper makes a
profit and in this sense can be said to report the news "for purposes
of trade," judicial constructions of the New York statute establish beyond doubt that its enactment was not intended to interfere with the
legitimate dissemination of news. A person's right of privacy, therefore, does not extend to preventing the use of his or her name in
publishing the news.

The General Interest Exception

Another broad exception to the statute allows the publication of
material on subjects of general interest to the public. These topics—a
few examples would be trends in fashion, manners, the arts—are not
"hot news" but are nonetheless legitimately of interest to the public,
and names and likenesses of individuals connected with them may
be used without prior written consent. Names and photographs of
such individuals, unless they bear no relationship whatever to the
subject matter or are acquired through some type of intrusion, may,
generally speaking, be used under the "general interest" exception
without consent and will not make the publisher liable for misappropriation. (Some cases analyze the use of real people in a fictionalization of actual events under the rubric of misappropriation. Those
cases are discussed below under "false light.")

The principle underlying the news and general interest exceptions
springs from the First Amendment theory that our system of
self-government and ordered liberties is best protected by the widest
possible dissemination of speech and ideas. Indeed, New York's
courts have shown an awareness that the statute would be unconstitutional without the news and general interest exceptions.

Using Names in Ads

The statute does work to prohibit the misappropriation of an individual's name or likeness in pure advertising. Thus, if an automobile
manufacturer were to utilize the name of a famous or obscure citizen
in an advertising campaign as an endorsement of its newest car without that person's consent, a misappropriation would have occurred.

Publishers, however, do have a limited right to use, without consent, the names and photographs of even famous people who have
appeared in their publications in advertising promoting those publications. In one case, *Booth v. Curtis Publishing Company* (1962),
Holiday magazine's advertisement reproduced a photograph and description of the actress Shirley Booth, taken from an article which

had appeared earlier in its editorial pages in connection with her attendance at the opening of a new resort hotel. In another case, *Namath v. Time Inc.* (1976), *Sports Illustrated* magazine utilized a photograph of Joe Namath in action at the Super Bowl, which had previously been published in the magazine; also, his name appeared prominently in the text of the advertisement. In neither case had the plaintiffs consented to these uses, and in neither case did the court find an invasion of privacy. The reasoning endorsed by New York's highest court was that these uses were not prohibited by the statute since they, like "news uses" and "general interest uses," were merely "incidental" to the dissemination of news. Consequently, so long as the names and likenesses have been previously published editorially and are utilized in advertising only to "illustrate the quality and content" of the publication, no written consent is necessary and no misappropriation has occurred.

Naturally, it may well be a question of degree whether a particular use of a name or likeness is "merely incidental"; a court may find that misappropriation has occurred where an advertisement implies an endorsement of the magazine by the individual depicted in it. Accordingly, the court in *Cher v. Forum International, Ltd.* (1982) decided that a misappropriation of the well-known entertainer's name occurred when *Forum* ran an advertisement stating that Cher had revealed information in an interview with *Forum* that she would not have revealed to *People* or *Us* magazines. Cher had given the interview to a freelancer who had originally intended to publish it in *Us*. The magazine was held liable for the advertisement's false implication of Cher's endorsement of *Forum*. In the absence of an implied endorsement by the individual, however, it can be said that publications have a limited privilege to utilize an individual's name and likeness in their own promotional activities without prior consent.

False Light

This third privacy right states that the publication of nondefamatory but untrue information about an individual, information that places him or her in a "false light" before the public, is an invasion of privacy. The false light in which the individual is placed must be highly offensive to a reasonable person, although many courts pay little attention to this requirement. It is difficult to pinpoint the precise theoretical basis of this injurious act. In one sense it can be likened to common law libel since it alleges that an injury occurs through the publication of untrue information. In another sense, it may simply be a misappropriation of an individual's *name*, which, since the account in which it appears is false, is not privileged as being incidental to the system of news dissemination. Indeed, cases involving fictionalization of actual events are sometimes labeled as "misappropriation" cases, and sometimes as "false light" cases.

Mixing Fact and Fiction Dangerous

Regardless of the label applied, a living person may be able to recover for invasion of privacy if his or her name or likeness is used without permission in an intentionally fictionalized account of a real-life story. Thus, in *Spahn v. Julian Messner, Inc.* (1967), Warren Spahn, a well-known baseball player, sued over the publication of an unauthorized biography, alleging that his rights under the New York misappropriation statute had been invaded. The court held that the author's pervasive use of literary techniques such as "invented dialogue, imaginary incidents and attributed thoughts and feelings" amounted to a misappropriation of the plaintiff's persona.

The U.S. Supreme Court has made it clear, however, that invasion of privacy claims challenging fictionalization of real-life events are limited by the freedom of speech and press guarantees of the First Amendment. In a leading case, *Time Inc. v. Hill*, *Life* magazine had reported the opening of a Broadway production, *The Desperate Hours*, which was an adaptation of a novel based substantially on the true story of a family who had been taken hostage in their home by escaped convicts. The magazine article depicted the family as the historical antecedents of the characters in the play, and it was arguably stated that the play reenacted the family's experience. Moreover, the article did not clearly identify certain episodes in the drama as fictitious. In these ways, the family alleged, they were portrayed in a false light before the public.

The Supreme Court reversed the trial court award of damages on the ground that damages cannot be awarded for an invasion of privacy arising out of the report of a matter of interest to the public (here, the Broadway opening), unless it can be proved that the untrue material was published "with knowledge of falsity or reckless disregard for the truth." This is, of course, the familiar "actual malice" standard the Court had earlier imposed in libel cases on plaintiffs who are public figures. The same limitations were necessary in privacy cases, the Court reasoned, in order to ensure that freedoms of expression "have the breathing space that they need to survive."

In a more recent case, *Cantrell v. Forest City Publishing Co.* (1974), the Court's task was to determine, in line with *Hill*, whether the false information at issue had been published with knowledge of falsity or reckless disregard for the truth. In the case, a newspaper carried a follow-up feature article about a family whose husband and father had perished some months earlier in a widely publicized bridge accident. The widow claimed that the follow-up article placed her in a false light because, among other things, it falsely implied that she had been present during the reporter's visit to the family home (in fact, only some of the children had been present) and that he had observed her wearing the "same mask of nonexpression" she had worn at her husband's funeral. The presence of such "calculated falsehoods" in the story led the Court to uphold a jury verdict that the plaintiff had been portrayed in a false light through knowing or reckless untruth.

Reconstructing Dialogue

The intentional use of falsehood in *Spahn* and *Cantrell* can be distinguished from the use of "reconstructed" dialogue, a technique that has become commonplace in recent years. This technique was used extensively, for example, in David McClintock's book *Indecent Exposure*, which was about the David Begelman check-forging scandal in Hollywood. So long as such dialogue is based on solid research and is informed by the actual facts, it should not be an invasion of privacy. Similarly, recent privacy and libel cases indicate that "docudramas" about public figures are protected by the actual malice standard. As one court put it, a docudrama "self-evidently . . . partakes of author's license—it is a creative interpretation of reality." That case was a libel suit brought against the makers of *Missing*, a film based on a true story about the disappearance of a young American in Chile. The court noted that the alterations made to dramatize the actual events depicted did not "distort the fundamental story being told" and dismissed the action, concluding that "[in] docudrama, minor fictionalization cannot be considered evidence or support for the requirement of actual malice."

Public Disclosure of Private and Embarrassing Facts

Public disclosure privacy holds that an individual's privacy may be invaded merely by the publication of private and embarrassing facts concerning that individual if the matter publicized is not of legitimate concern to the public and would be highly offensive to a reasonable person. An aggrieved party may recover even if the report is entirely truthful. Moreover, recovery for the wrongful act does not depend upon the presence of intrusive gathering of information, as the injury occurs with the publication of the private and embarrassing facts, however acquired. Public disclosure privacy provides a most direct clash with the act of publishing, arraying as it does First Amendment privileges for truthful expression against a right to keep secrets which many people would agree deserves protection.

Newsworthy Facts Can Be Printed

Public disclosure claims are rarely successful. In general, if the court finds that the disclosure of private facts is "newsworthy" the claim will fail. The standard for newsworthiness was examined in *Virgil v. Time Inc.* (1976). At issue in that leading case was the publication of various truthful incidents from the plaintiff's past which were offered as an explanation of his daredevil prowess at bodysurfing at a particularly dangerous spot in southern California. The alleged private and embarrassing facts—such as that Virgil extinguished cigarettes in his mouth to impress women, intentionally injured himself in order to collect unemployment so as to have time for bodysurfing, ate insects—were revealed to the *Sports Illustrated* reporter by the bodysurfer, but the surfer later forbade publication of such incidents prior to the publication of the article.

The court in *Virgil* held that the plaintiff's suit was without merit and granted summary judgment for the defendant. Recognizing that truthful disclosures are privileged under the First Amendment if they are "newsworthy," the court stated two conditions which must be met in order to lose this constitutional protection. First, the facts must be highly offensive as a matter of community mores, and these were not: "The facts themselves . . . are not sufficiently offensive to reach the very high level of offensiveness necessary . . . to lose newsworthiness protection. . . . The above facts are generally unflattering and perhaps embarrassing, but they are simply not offensive to the degree of morbidity and sensationalism."

Even if the disclosures had shown the requisite offensiveness, the plaintiff was unable to satisfy the second requirement, that the revelation of the facts be for its own sake: "Both parties agree that bodysurfing at the Wedge is a legitimate public interest, and it cannot be doubted that the plaintiff Mike Virgil's unique prowess at the same is also of legitimate public interest. Any reasonable person reading the *Sports Illustrated* article would have to conclude that the personal facts concerning Mike Virgil were included as a legitimate journalistic attempt to explain Virgil's extremely daring and dangerous style of bodysurfing at the Wedge. There is no possibility that a juror could conclude that the personal facts were included for any inherent, morbid, sensational, or curiosity appeal they might have." In finding *Sports Illustrated's* article a legitimate journalistic exercise, the court concluded "that there is a rational and at least arguably close relationship between the facts revealed and the activity to be explained." But, it hastened to add, its opinion "should not be read as in any way endorsing no-holds-barred rummaging by the media through the private lives of persons engaged in activities of public interest under the pretense of elucidating that activity or the person's participation in it."

Using Facts from Public Records

An important defense to public disclosure claims holds that there can be no penalty for publishing information that is obtained from a public record. This defense was established in the decision of the United States Supreme Court in *Cox Broadcasting v. Cohn*, decided in 1975. In that case, the father of a murdered rape victim sued a television station for invasion of his privacy when it broadcast her name, in violation of a state statute prohibiting the revelation of the name of a rape victim, in a report on the sentencing of the rapists. It was held that no invasion of privacy had occurred because the victim's name had been obtained from judicial records that were open to public inspection: "The commission of crime, prosecutions resulting from it, and judicial proceeding arising from the prosecutions . . . are without question events of legitimate concern to the public and consequently fall within the responsibility of the press to report the operations of government." In effect, the information was not private at all.

Disclosing Distant Pasts

When private facts relate to events in an individual's distant past, courts may afford the defendant less latitude. There is some authority permitting successful lawsuits for private disclosure of an individual's criminal past where the individual has reformed in the intervening years. For example, in *Melvin v. Reid* (1931) a motion picture accurately portrayed the public testimony of the plaintiff as a witness in a murder trial seven years before. The plaintiff's testimony established that she had been a prostitute but had since entered respectable society. The court held that under the circumstances, the facts of these incidents (which were a matter of public record) were newsworthy but the names of the participants were not.

Historical facts relating to persons who are public officials or public figures, however, do not easily become private with the passage of time, as demonstrated by *Sidis v. F-R Publishing Corp.* (1940). The *New Yorker* magazine in 1937 published a biographical sketch of the plaintiff, who had been a celebrated and much-publicized child prodigy in 1910. In the ensuing years, the plaintiff had chosen to seek obscurity and to conceal his past identity, and these efforts as well as various eccentricities of the plaintiff were detailed in the 1937 article. Although there was nothing untrue in the article, it was characterized by the court as "a ruthless exposure of a once public character, who has since sought and has now been deprived of the seclusion of private life."

Nonetheless, the article was held not to be an invasion of privacy. The plaintiff had once been a public figure, and the 1937 article was newsworthy in that it provided answers to the question whether the plaintiff had fulfilled his tremendous promise; hence, it was still a matter of public interest. The court recognized that some revelations might be so intimate and unwarranted as "to outrage the community's notions of decency. But when focused upon public characters, truthful comments upon dress, speech, habits, and the ordinary aspects of personality will usually not transgress this line."

Despite the generally favorable precedents in this branch of privacy law, particular facts of a case may move some courts to allow recovery. In *Hawkins v. Multimedia* (1980), which was decided by the highest state court in South Carolina, a newspaper published a story about teenage pregnancies which identified the plaintiff, a teenage boy, as the father of an illegitimate child. The reporter who spoke to the boy purported to be seeking information for survey purposes only and did not disclose that the plaintiff would be identified in the story. Despite the close connection between the private matters disclosed and the newsworthy subject matter of the article, the court affirmed a jury verdict against the newspaper. The court reasoned that while the right of privacy does not prohibit the publication of matters of legitimate public interest, public interest "does not mean mere curiosity, and newsworthiness is not necessarily the test." This rather unfelicitous view of newsworthiness was no doubt inspired, at least in part, by the age of the plaintiff and the court's disapproval of the conduct of the reporter.

Review/Chapter 2

The four types of invasion of privacy are:
✔intrusion
✔misappropriation of a person's name
✔publicity that places a person in a false light
✔publicity that discloses private and embarrassing facts

Some writers protect themselves from invasion of privacy claims by asking permission before taping a telephone call. However, this is not legally necessary if the call:
✔crosses state boundaries and is not made for an illegal purpose
✔or takes place in a state that permits one-party consent

You should obtain a person's permission before using his or her name in an advertisement. However, generally speaking, publishers can use a person's name or photograph without permission in an advertisement for the publication if:
✔the name or likeness has been previously published editorially in the publication advertised
✔is used only to illustrate the quality and content of the publication
✔and does not imply an endorsement of the publication by the individual pictured

Disclosing facts that are true but embarrassing is generally protected if:
✔the story is of legitimate public interest
✔and the facts are not highly offensive

Chapter 3
Avoiding Libel Suits

Michael S. Lasky

Libel—it's one of the most dreaded words in a writer's vocabulary. A successful suit can destroy a writer's reputation and bring financial ruin. Even winning a libel suit can be expensive and damaging, so the best approach is to avoid a suit. This chapter tells how:

1. Most publications check stories for potentially libelous material.

2. The courts have defined "public figures" and the requirement that they show "actual malice" to win a libel suit.

3. Photographs, captions, headlines, and illustrations can be libelous.

4. The use of corrections and words such as "alleged" may not help, but getting the subject's permission or a refusal to comment may.

5. Some subjects are more likely than others to result in suits.

You may never have been sued for libel. You may never have even thought of being sued. But an action for libel can come from anywhere at anytime from anyone.

As with any law that deals with what is "truth," the subtleties and nuances create particular problems of their own. In libel cases, it is not only the letter of the law with which the writer and editor must be concerned but also *where* the law is written. There are fifty different libel laws—one for each state. Despite this fact, the basic common law tenets of libel law philosophy upon which state laws are based are unwavering, and it is a risky business indeed to misunderstand these tenets. The State of New York defines libel as: "A malicious publication which exposes any living person or the memory of any person deceased, to hatred, contempt, ridicule or obloquy, or which causes, or tends to cause any person to be shunned or avoided, or which has a tendency to injure any person, corporation or association of persons, in his or their business or occupation, is a libel." (New York Consolidated Laws, 1909—no revisions since.)

Three Elements of Libel

If any of the following three elements is missing, there is no libel.

Defamation—Generally defined as injury to reputation, it must apply to an identifiable person and it must be published.

Identification—Unless the plaintiff can prove that the defamatory meaning actually applies to that individual, there is no libel. A third party must understand that the reference is to the plaintiff whether by nickname, pseudonym, or circumstance.

Publication—Printing, posting, or circulating are the first steps in publication of a libel; someone reading the message is the second step. Most courts subscribe to what is called the *single publication rule.* This means an entire edition of a newspaper or magazine is treated as a single publication of one copy, rather than every single copy constituting a separate case of libel.

Preventive Journalism

Most magazine publishers follow a course of preventive rather than corrective efforts in dealing with libel. That is, they prefer to stay out of court rather than to win a lawsuit.

At *New York* magazine, which prides itself on its crusading journalism, former editor Sheldon Zalaznick (now with *Forbes*) points out that the magazine meticulously researches articles and that particularly controversial pieces are "lawyered" from start to finish.

"There is no substitute for first rate counsel," he says. "The magazine's attorney views articles in three ways. After reading the story under scrutiny he will say 'this is libelous' or 'you're home free' or 'this is defensible.' The last is not to say the story might invite a lawsuit but that it could be defended if necessary. This is where the hard to-publish-or-not-to-publish judgments come and where the prospect of a costly court battle looms."

For even if you take your case to court and win, the magazine still has to pay the combat expenses. Libel cases that reach court are usually pyrrhic victories for publications, at best.

New York once published a sensational account on the dubious practices of some New York doctors. The physicians' names were removed reluctantly at press time, recalls Zalaznick. "Our lawyer said that while it was defensible, the doctors would feel obliged to sue us just for the record—so that they would have something to tell their patients and the medical association."

Known for its outspoken and provocative writing ("The 10 Worst Judges in N.Y.," "Radical Chic"), *New York* will send its writers to attorneys even before they start writing. A firm grasp of libel law as it may affect the piece the writer is about to tackle can save them in later research, *New York* has found.

Even after the "lawyered" article is written, the editors, aided by a host of researchers, will go through the piece flagging what is thought to need further corroboration. "I will literally ask the author to come to the office with his or her notes and files and prove the accuracy of what is said in the article. Occasionally a staff researcher will venture beyond what the writer offers for substantiation.

"In my 'primer' of things to do," says Zalaznick, "I think that first, you get a good lawyer. Without a good lawyer, you are nowhere. An overly cautious lawyer will usually take the viewpoint of the plaintiff instead of the publication. Next you check context and phraseology. Sometimes it is not what you say but how, in the context of the story, you say it. And third in my primer, take special care in editing and checking before the article is sent to the printer."

After a suit occurs, editors are usually the first to see points they realize they should have caught but somehow missed. Many times, however, the editor isn't culpable for libel actions.

As noted libel attorney Douglas Hamilton points out, "It's hard to forecast where libel actions are going to grow—on what branches they are going to grow—because most of them come from articles and statements from sources you can't prevent." Sometimes a libel action will emerge from a coincidental event that could not be predicted but which changes the nature of the facts as they appear in a story.

The classic case of a simple birth announcement demonstrates this. A newspaper reported the birth of Mrs. Smith's baby. It was during World War II, however, and Mr. Smith had not been home for several years—even on a furlough. It was therefore physically impossible for the baby to be his child. The woman sued because of the resulting verbal abuse the announcement caused.

One of the best ways to prevent libel in all situations, according to Hamilton, is to get in touch with the "victim" of the article and get his or her side.

"It's the best insurance I can think of," he submits.

Truth as a Defense

The other universal defense against libel is, simply, the truth. It is the writer's sword, but it is also his or her shield.

Determining the truth in the context of a magazine story can be a fine-grained problem. A magazine's prerogative to expand upon the facts and offer interpretation and analysis to readers is usually the place where libel is born.

Harold Hayes, former editor of *Esquire*, explains that this monthly magazine approaches observational and interpretative journalism with a keen eye and a pointed pencil. "You must have evidence to justify your interpretation," Hayes states. "A magazine should be able to document sufficiently whatever interpretation it is going to make . . . if it goes beyond what the evidence suggests, it would be my responsibility to restrict the degree of the author's comment."

Truth Is Not Always a Cure

The dichotomy between accurate reporting and truth must be emphasized. Accuracy, according to the courts, is not enough. You can accurately report some false charge or fact that is libelous.

It is *how* you treat and present the truth that ascertains whether you have published libel.

Because of the very nature of the journalistic profession, it is often difficult to prove that you printed the truth.

The dilemma stems from an entirely different issue now being bandied about in the courts—the question of the privilege of the reporter. Central to these current cases—most of them involving newspaper reporters—is the debate over whether a reporter has the right to keep the sources confidential. These cases are closely connected with libel actions.

To get vital information a writer often must agree to keep his or her sources anonymous. If journalists were to open up their confidential files to legislative investigation, grand juries, and courts, the basic First Amendment freedom, it is argued, would be violated, as would the sources.

Thus, truth, as revealed in a story, frequently cannot be used in a defense. But the privilege of reporting, insured by the Constitution, can be.

This right is interpreted by the courts to be held by anyone—not just the press. It supplies immunity from libel damages for objective reports on events of public interest. These range from commonplace news conferences to court proceedings to daily news coverage. The only conditions to this defense are that the article in question be a *report* that is *balanced* (fair) and *accurate* (true).

Public Officials Must Prove Malice

Just as the editorial copy in a publication must be clean, so, too, must the advertising. The rule stems from an action brought against the *New York Times* in 1960. An advertisement for the Committee to Defend Martin Luther King and the Struggle for Freedom in the South appeared in the *Times* in March 1960. Five libel suits based on this ad and totaling some $3 million were filed. One of the first cases tried in the Alabama courts was that of L. B. Sullivan, commissioner of public affairs for Montgomery.

While not mentioned by name, Sullivan felt that the word "police" referred to him and that the public knew it, because they knew he was in charge of the police.

The case was first decided in favor of the commissioner for the full $500,000 in damages that he demanded.

The *Times* appealed to the Supreme Court who in 1964 decided in favor of the *Times*.

The Court said that the rule would apply only when the libel concerned the official's public conduct and the remarks were not a knowing lie or reckless disregard of the truth.

The *New York Times* rule, as it is now called, "prohibits a public official from recovering damages from a defamatory falsehood relating to his official conduct unless he proves that the statement was made with 'actual malice,' that is, with knowledge that it was false or with reckless disregard of whether it was false or not."

Subsequent cases that reached the Supreme Court have enabled the justices to expand upon the *Times* rule and allow even more leeway for the print media to publish freely.

Rule Applies to All Public Interest Stories

In 1966, the Court enlarged upon the *Times* rule and said it extended not only to public officials but to all people or events in the *public interest*. The extension was the result of *Time Inc. v. Hill*. This case began back in 1955 when *Life* magazine published a picture story about the opening of a play entitled "The Desperate Hours" based on a novel of the same title. The article claimed that the play was a reenactment of the experiences of the James Hill family who three years earlier were held captive by three escaped convicts. Hill sued, claiming *Life* invaded his family's privacy. In the lower courts, Hill was awarded $30,000, but when the case reached the Supreme Court, a new interpretation of the law favored Time Inc.

The Court said that if the press was saddled with the "impossible burden of verifying to a certainty the facts associated in an article with a person's name, picture or portrait," it would no longer be free. "Fear of large verdicts in damage suits for innocent or more negligent misstatement, even fear of the expense involved in their defense," it was submitted, "would diminish the power of an effective press."

In 1976, however, the Supreme Court restricted the broad protection given the press against libel suits brought by "public figures." In *Time Inc. v. Firestone*, the Supreme Court limited its definition of public figures, and subjected reporters and publishers to libel judgments for misreporting court decisions, even when a news story is "a rational interpretation of an ambiguous document." The Firestone case came to the courts as a result of an inaccurate *Time* magazine account of the divorce proceedings of Mrs. Firestone. Although Firestone is a well-known name in Palm Beach society, the courts decided she was not a "public figure" (as defined by the *The New York Times* rule) for the purposes of deciding how much constitutional protection could be allowed a publisher in misreporting a court proceeding.

What Is Malice?

In *Times v. Sullivan*, the Court cautioned that "calculated falsehoods" do not enjoy the constitutional protection afforded to information that contributes to the exposition of ideas.

What is considered reckless disregard of the truth was made clear in 1967 when the High Court decided against the *Saturday Evening Post* in its appeal of a $360,000 libel verdict handed down in 1963.

In the March 23, 1963, issue of the *Post*, it was alleged that Wallace Butts, then the University of Georgia's athletic director, gave information about Georgia players and strategy to Paul (Bear) Bryant, a University of Alabama coach.

The libelous story said that an insurance salesman had accidentally been cut into a telephone conversation between Butts and Bryant. The magazine's conclusion was clearly that Butts and Bryant had conspired to fix the outcome of the game.

Editor Clay Blair Jr. claimed the *Post* was following a policy of "sophisticated muckraking." While muckraking might be a praiseworthy venture, it is safe from a claim of libel only when the muck is true.

The jury decided that the *Post*'s journalism was not so sophisticated. An inaccurate date, an unattributable quote, and other flaws demonstrated the "reckless disregard of the truth."

The Supreme Court conceded that Butts as a public official came under the *Times* rule, but added that the malice of the story did also.

Malice is not considered *fair comment*, another avenue of defense. Used primarily when matters of opinion in columns, reviews, letters to the editor, and other comments of a critical nature are in question, *fair comment* hinges on the following criteria:

- The libelous comment must be an opinion—not statement of fact.
- The opinion must be fair.
- There must be no malice.
- The opinion must rest on the facts.

As the *Saturday Evening Post* case proved, hefty awards can be made if libel is found.

Damages

Damages represent a triple threat to the publisher.

Compensatory damages are given for injury to reputation. When libel is found to exist, damage is presumed and the jury must decide the amount of the award. The court may review the jury's award and lower the amount if it is out of proportion to the injury suffered. The plaintiff does not have to even show damages.

The second threat is *special* damages which represent the actual pecuniary loss suffered because of the libel. Here the victim must prove damages precisely.

The third and final danger to the publisher's coffers comes in the guise of *punitive* damages—sometimes called "smut money." These damages are designed to punish past libel and discourage any future malice. The courts define actual malice as "knowledge of falsity or a high degree of awareness of probable falsity at the time of publication." Libel law in its evolution over time now places the burden on the plaintiff to allege *and prove* the statements of which he complains are false.

Thus, when the *Saturday Evening Post* lost, the jury at first awarded $3 million in punitive damages. (This was reduced by the judge to $400,000.) As one member of the jury summed up its motives:

"We wanted the public to know that we would not condone that kind of journalism and we wanted it in unmistakable terms to keep the *Post* from doing the same thing to someone else, maybe in a high place."

For this reason alone, newsweeklies such as *Newsweek, Time,* and *Business Week* go to great lengths to check and recheck a story before it is published.

A Time Inc. staff attorney notes that all its magazines make reasonable efforts to ascertain the accuracy of what is said *before* publication. While there is no particular order to researching stories, a reporter will submit anything questionable to the legal department before proceeding. Because of *Time's* deadline, a fair amount of material is summarily forwarded to the lawyers from the editors, writers, and researchers. The legal department will return the material in question to researchers or writers for further clarification or corroboration.

At *Business Week*, an editor explains that "accuracy is more important than interpretation and style. We edit for fairness first."

Rules May Differ for Magazines

How a publication is classified—as a magazine or newspaper—can also determine whether libel laws apply to what it publishes. When Carol Burnett sued the *National Enquirer* in 1976 about an incident that never occurred but which the *Enquirer* reported on, the *Enquirer* tried to have her claim set aside based on a California "retraction statute." The statute exempts a newspaper or broadcasting station that publishes or broadcasts a correction of the offending defamation. The court ruled that the *Enquirer* was a magazine despite its claim of being a newspaper. The court said that the content and non-deadline nature of the *National Enquirer* made it a magazine, not a newspaper.

While the Burnett case did not change libel laws, when the jury found in her favor, it did raise the question of just how far celebrities must surrender their private lives to public scrutiny. The jury decided that the *Enquirer* had indeed acted recklessly in publishing a gossip item about a defamatory incident it knew did not occur.

Libel Insurance

Libel insurance is available to publishers from a few insurance companies.

The criteria usually used to calculate premiums are based on the particular publication—its circulation, frequency, content, history, and other factors.

Firms such as Employers Reinsurance Corporation of Overland Park, Kansas, and Media/Professional Insurance, Inc. of Kansas City, Missouri, offer libel insurance to publishers but it is usually not available to freelance writers. Authors may on occasion be covered by agreements with their publishers.

Who Takes the Blame—Editor or Writer?

Unlike other news magazines, *Business Week* requires that reporters be responsible for the final accuracy test. Even if a story goes through to the editors, it is returned for final OK by the reporter.

"Cutting can lead to distortions and context changes," says an editor. "The original reporter can correct this."

While the reporter is checking the veracity of the story, the editor must always be concerned with whether a story, however true, is defensible.

The editor is the troubleshooter. He or she weighs the risks of publishing the story—and the value of those risks. The editor examines the stature of the sources for reliability and/or prestige. He or she analyzes whether a story is defensible enough to still be worth publishing.

But even when these editorial judgments are made correctly, there are still pitfalls for the editor.

Two Problem Areas

Two other problem areas should be noted. First is the creation of a headline, and second, the selection of illustrations or photographs.

Sometimes headlines can be libelous, especially when they vary from what the content of the story suggests. One has only to look as far as some of the provocative catchlines used in movie fan magazines to see libelous discrepancies between what the headlines suggest and what the stories really say.

A headline should get reader attention—not a libel suit. The best way to avoid litigation from a head is for the editor to create it on the basis of the concrete facts of the story and not what the story *suggests.*

Pictures should also match the story they illustrate.

Photographs can defame people, whether they were intended for the story or misplaced with another. When a newspaper ran a photo of a woman (who was identified as a bride-to-be) holding a baby in her arms, it lost $500. The bride sued because of the ensuing shame she was subjected to among her friends. The picture was obviously misplaced, but occasionally even ones that are properly set to an article can be dangerous.

The way a photo is cropped or captioned can change the meaning of it. And if an author does not want to actually identify the target of a possibly libelous story, a picture should not show any details that would help identify the person.

Illustrations that make the subject look foolish to others can be libelous also. Yet the editor should not be paranoid in selection. Photos and other artwork are covered under the "fair comment" doctrine, and courts broadly interpret libel law when dealing with photos, according to attorneys.

Fiction Can Cause Friction

Just because words are labeled "fiction" does not protect them from potential libel actions. Ask novelist Gwen Davis Mitchell, whose novel, *Touching*, was the object of a successful claim by Paul Bindrim, Ph.D., a licensed clinical psychologist. Bindrim ran nude encounter groups, which he proved were grossly portrayed in the novel.

Mitchell had attended one of Bindrim's sessions and signed a standard agreement not to write about it. For her part, Mitchell wanted to knock what she thought to be a dangerous form of psychological therapy so she created a devastating portrait of the fictional character based on Bindrim.

The case demonstrated that if a writer wants to comment about loosely disguised real people, the libel laws are not waived because the commentary is packaged as fiction. The writer must create characters that are not reasonably identifiable as actual persons while still relaying the truths about the disguised reality the writer wants to show. (See Chapter Four for more on fiction and libel.)

Corrections Won't Keep You Out of Court

Even if a newspaper or magazine publishes a correction of an error brought to its attention, it is not completely off the hook in the courtroom.

Corrections are only a partial defense proving goodwill on the part of the publisher. It helps to show that there was no intended malice.

The word "alleged" does not keep a publication free from liability. It is necessary, then, to be able to prove what happened *did* happen or attribute the reporting of the event to an official source. Editors have found that when possible, submitting the manuscript to the subject for review of inaccuracies—but not revisions in the text itself—may avoid the risk of libel.

Consent of the victim to publish a story is an absolute defense. Refusal to comment when approached by the publication will also help the publication's defense of a libel case.

The single most overriding factor causing defamation lawsuits for publications is, according to lawyer Douglas Hamilton, "editors' carelessness."

While most editors are aware of the dangers of libel, slip-ups can be prevented. If a standard thought process is consciously used by editor and writer alike, chances are that they will prevent libel every time.

Three Questions Editors Should Ask

The three-pronged approach that could be used is:
- Is the material defamatory to an identifiable individual or group?
- If it *is*, then, is the information privileged?
- If it *is not*, then, is it fundamentally true?

Even though the answer to the last question may be yes, that does not mean the piece should be published. One more question must be asked. Would the target feel obligated to sue to demonstrate denial of the libel? If so, the publisher must weigh the worth of publication versus risk of possible court expenses.

If you can establish some kind of reflex-like routine for watching what you say in your manuscript before publication, you will have gone a long way toward keeping the libel wolf away from your door. Sometimes even that will not be enough.

Some Subjects Tricky

Ariel Sharon v. Time Magazine proved that sometimes libel suits are more a forum of political ideology than actual claims against writers or publications. Sharon is the former Minister of Defense of Israel who sued *Time* over a February 1983 article about an Israeli Commission report on the findings of an inquiry into the events that led to the massacre of unarmed Palestinians in West Beirut refugee camps. The article included a statement that, "Sharon also reportedly discussed with the Gemayels the need for the Phalangists to take revenge for the assassination of Bashir, but the details of this conversation are not known." Sharon and his attorneys claimed this statement implied Sharon "condoned" or "instigated" the massacre.

Time claimed it based the statement on information from high sources who had knowledge of an unpublished section of the commission report. Sharon charged *Time* with "blood libel"—a historical tool of anti-Semitism—and thus made his case more a political action than a legal one.

Time's position was complicated because the reporter's sources were confidential, so researchers could not check to see how accurate the information was before the article was printed.

The judge asked the jury three questions it had to answer, each asked and answered before proceeding to the next:
1. Did Sharon prove that the *Time* story defamed him with its implications? YES.
2. Did Sharon prove he had not engaged in any discussion with Phalangists about the need for revenge? YES.

3. Did *Time* have serious doubts about the truth of the false and defamatory statement when it was published—using the *New York Times* "reckless disregard" rule?

The jury said NO, *Time* had not acted recklessly or with malice but believed its story was correct.

Time said it had learned about a fact it had only *inferred* based on information from its sources. While the *New York Times* rule protects this behavior, it does not prevent the expense of the lawsuit it may trigger.

The *Sharon v. Time* case demonstrates that with controversial subjects, particularly those concerning deeply felt political beliefs, the writer must be particularly careful to ascertain the truth, and that reliance on "trusted sources" can be expensive.

Review/Chapter 3

The three elements necessary for a statement to be considered libelous are:
> the person must be defamed
> the person must be identified so that a third party can understand who is referred to
> the statement must be circulated to others

A public figure cannot recover damages for libel unless the statement was made with "actual malice," which is defined as either:
> knowledge the statement was false
> or reckless disregard of whether it was false

One defense against libel is that the statement was "fair comment." The criteria for the fair comment defense are:
> the statement must be an opinion, not a statement of fact
> the opinion must be fair
> there must be no malice
> the opinion must rest on the facts

Photographs can be libelous, too. Some of the most common mistakes are photos that:
> are accidentally printed with the wrong story or caption
> have been cropped or shot in such a way that they distort the situation or change its meaning
> show details that identify a person who was to have been mentioned anonymously

If you are sued for libel, it may help if you can show that you:
> used qualifying words such as "alleged" and can attribute the statements to an official source
> asked the subject to comment and the subject refused
> published a correction retracting any incorrect information as soon as the mistake was identified

Chapter 4
Fiction Can Be Dangerous, Too!

Carol E. Rinzler

Fiction writers sometimes think they're immune from suits accusing them of libel or invasion of privacy. After all, they're writing about people they made up, so who could be hurt—right? Wrong. This chapter will tell you what the dangers are so you can avoid them, as well as how suits involving fiction differ from those involving nonfiction. It covers:

1. How closely a fictional character must resemble a real person for that person to sue successfully.

2. Whether efforts to disguise a character based on a real person, such as changing the character's name and introducing different characteristics, help.

3. Why authors benefit from a requirement that a plaintiff prove that readers believed the fictionalized account was true.

Two decades after the landmark decisions of *Times v. Sullivan* and *Time v. Hill*, authors still puzzle with the questions those cases have left us, among them what legal risks does the author of fiction run?

Many lawyers date their troubles in the area of fiction to *Bindrim v. Mitchell*, better known as the Gwen Davis case, decided in 1979. In that case, Dr. Paul Bindrim, a California psychologist, sued author Gwen Davis Mitchell and Doubleday, her publisher, claiming he had been libeled by her portrayal of him as a character in the bestseller *Touching*. The novel's Dr. Simon Herford was a California psychiatrist who ran nude encounter groups that were characterized by their leader's "crude, aggressive, and unprofessional conduct," and resulted in the death of one participant, so upset after a session she cracked up her car. Bindrim did, in fact, run nude encounter groups that had led to no deaths, which Davis surely should have known, Bindrim argued, because she had attended a marathon's worth herself. Doubleday and Davis maintained that no reasonable reader would identify Bindrim as Herford—the two were physically dissimilar, Herford was a psychiatrist and Bindrim a psychologist, and, because a dozen or more nude encounter groups flourished in California, Bindrim was not identifiable simply because he was unique. Nevertheless, the court awarded damages of $50,000 against Davis and Doubleday and an additional $25,000 in punitive damages against the publisher.

The publicity surrounding Bindrim may have focused publishers' attention on a problem they had been too blithe about, but the case was hardly the first in which a fictionalized figure sued. In 1934, Princess Irina Yousoupoff proved to the satisfaction of an English court that she was identifiable as Princess Natasha in the movie *Rasputin: The Mad Monk.* (The defamatory statement was that the princess had been raped by Rasputin; MGM's argument that the statement wasn't libelous provoked from the Lord Justice the comment, "I really have no language to express my opinion of that argument.") In another early case, an upstanding New York magistrate named Corrigan recovered against Bobbs-Merrill, publishers of a "sensational novel" called *God's Man.* Judge Corrigan argued successfully that his portrayal as a New York judge named Cornigan "exposed him to hatred, contempt, ridicule and obloquy as being ignorant, brutal, hypocritical, corrupt, shunned by his fellows, bestial of countenance . . . and grossly unfit for his place."

Plaintiff Must Prove Identification

In short, the fact that it's fiction has never immunized a work from a libel or invasion-of-privacy suit. As the *Corrigan* court put it: "Reputations may not be traduced with impunity even under the literary form of a work of fiction." If a work is fiction, however, the law provides extra ammunition for shooting down a plaintiff.

Before a plaintiff can even start to prove that the material was defamatory, he has to prove that a "reasonable person would understand that the fictional character was, in actual fact, the plaintiff."

That most identifying of factors, a name, rarely has been sufficient by itself to prove identification, at least when the author chose the name inadvertently. Consider *Bernard Clare,* by James T. Farrell, the saga of an aspiring and unpublished writer and his "sordid experiences" in New York and Chicago. A Minneapolis newspaper and magazine writer named Bernard Clare sued for libel. If Bernard Clare was based on any real person, it was Farrell himself, and Farrell swore he'd chosen the name without any idea the plaintiff existed. (He wanted a name that sounded Irish, said Farrell.) The court, noting that "it is quite apparent from a reading of the book that it was intended as a work of fiction," that the author hadn't intended to portray the plaintiff, and that there were numerous differences between the real and fictional Clares, held for Farrell. A later court dealt similarly with *The Friends of Eddie Coyle.*

Disclaimers

The typical disclaimer, in which the author promises, among other things, that the work is fiction, is useful, if not talismanic, in staving off same-named plaintiffs. Consider the case of Marion Kerby, whose namesake was the heroine of a naughty 1939 Hal Roach film; in the course of promoting the movie, the studio conceived the clever idea of sending one thousand men a come-up-and-see-me-sometime note "on such stationery as women use in private correspondence . . . in pink envelopes addressed in a feminine hand," and signed, "Fondly, Your ectoplasmic playmate, Marion Kerby." Noting that the plaintiff was the only Marion Kerby in the Los Angeles telephone directory, the court focused on the fact that there was nothing in the note to "warn the reader that it was merely an advertisement or other work of fiction."

The use of fictional names in nonfiction can be a problem, especially if some but not all names have been changed. Barbara Gordon's *I'm Dancing As Fast as I Can* renamed an evil psychiatrist Dr. Allen and a real psychiatrist named Dr. Allen sued. A similar misfortune struck Susan Sheehan's *Is There No Place on Earth for Me?* The tricky circumstance of rechristening only some characters in a book may require a tricky disclaimer.

Fortunately, both Gordon and Sheehan won, as have most defendants in cases of this sort. If the reasoning of some decisions occasionally seems strained, the underlying policy is sensible. In the words of one judge: "To make accidental or coincidental use of a name a libel would impose a prohibitive burden upon authors, publishers and those who distribute the fruits of creative fancy. . . . It would be an astonishing doctrine if every writer of fiction were required to make a search among all the records available in this Nation which might tabulate the names and activities of millions of people in order to determine whether perchance one of the characters . . . may have the same name and occupation as a real person."

Disguising Characters

But what if the author really did base the character on the plaintiff, say the novelist whose main character and whose own older brother were both the same age, were both Latvian citizens, and were both the oldest son in a family of thirteen children who traveled around Europe in an old bus giving band and choir concerts with their father, a Russian Protestant minister? The lower court decided, without a trial, that the older brother wasn't identifiable; the appellate court said there should be a trial, a conclusion that might seem plain if it weren't for the fact that unless the writer has catalogued similarities of truly epic proportions between the character and the real person, the defendant probably will win.

Differences, even trivial ones, between a plaintiff and a fictional character provide a loophole through which a defendant can wriggle. In one case concerning a *Saturday Evening Post* short story, the plaintiff was named Larry Esco Middlebrooks; he was a friend from the author's boyhood in Columbia, S.C. The story featured an "Esco Brooks," a teenager who committed petty theft in that very town. But the court identified as "marked dissimilarities . . . the difference in ages, the absence of the plaintiff from Columbia at the time of the episode, and the differences in employment." Sympathizing with writers, the court wrote: "Authors of necessity must rely on their own background and experiences in writing fiction." Although several witnesses testified that they thought "Brooks" was Middlebrooks, the court dismissed their belief.

A Catch-22 for Plaintiffs

The most frequent, if tortured, judicial rationale protecting defendants is that anyone who knew the plaintiff well enough to think he was the character also knew the plaintiff well enough to know he wasn't. This approach reached its apogee in *Wheeler v. Dell Publishing Co.*, a 1962 case that concerned the novel *Anatomy of a Murder* and the subsequent movie of the same title. Hazel Wheeler, the widow of the actual murder victim, sued, arguing that the portrayal of Janice Quill, the fictional wife, defamed her; the character used "foul language," had an illegitimate child, and displayed "other unsavory characteristics." Despite a raft of similarities, the court concluded: "Those who knew she was [the victim's] widow . . . could not reasonably identify her with Janice Quill, for Hazel Wheeler denies having any of the specific 'unsavory characteristics' of Janice Quill."

In *Springer v. Viking Press* (1983), the court adopted much the same reasoning. The novel was *State of Grace* by Robert Tyne, and the plaintiff shared with the objectionable character the first name of Lisa, an identical physical description, and an apartment on West 114th Street in Manhattan. Unlike plaintiff Lisa Springer, however, the novel's Lisa Blake was a world-class call girl who had used her ill-gotten gains to abandon West 114th Street for a Fifth Avenue co-op. Blake's appearance in the novel was the occasion for a chapter's worth of graphic sex. Despite evidence that at least one reader had made the connection, the court found the similarities "in large part superficial" and the "dissimilarities both in manner of living and in outlook . . . so profound that it is virtually impossible to see how anyone who knew Springer could attribute to Springer the lifestyle of Lisa Blake." The dissenting judge pointed out: "The dissimilarities which the court stresses . . . are the very basis for the allegations of defamation." Or, as another court put it in another case: "The disturbing irony [is that] the more virtuous the victim of the libel, the less likely it will be that she will be able to establish [identification]. Thus, the more deserving the plaintiff of recompense for the tarnishing of a spotless reputation, the less likely will be any actual recovery."

As comforting as *Middlebrooks, Wheeler,* and *Springer* may be to authors, lawyers are wary of relying heavily on them as a fail-safe counterweight to *Bindrim.* The reasoning used by the courts, carried to its logical conclusion, means there never can be identification.

Even a plaintiff who can prove identification as a fictional character has a distance to go. The person who sues for invasion of privacy, for instance, can't recover in many states, including New York, unless his or her actual name has been used. Such was the fate of Carmen Wojtowicz, who sued for her fictional portrayal as the wife of the transsexual bank robber in *Dog Day Afternoon,* and of a man on whom John Hersey modeled a character in *A Bell for Adano.* The same was the lot of one Joseph Anthony Maggio, who sued Scribners for his alleged portrayal in James Jones's *From Here to Eternity* as Angelo Maggio. "The word 'name,' " wrote the court, referring to the New York statute, "means a person's full name and not merely his surname." Even though there was evidence that James Jones and others had known Joseph Anthony as "Angelo," Maggio lost.

Believability Also a Factor

Libel plaintiffs who prove the material is about them must also be able to prove that readers will believe the defamatory statements are statements of fact, often a difficult task. Consider the case of *Pring v. Penthouse,* over a short story about a Miss Wyoming whose talent was baton twirling and who performed fellatio upon her coach at the Miss America pageant, an act that caused the fellow to levitate. Kimerli Jayne Pring was, as it happened, a former Miss Wyoming, whose talent, as it happened, was baton twirling, and she sued *Penthouse* for libel. The jury awarded Pring a whopping $26 million, later reduced by the judge to $12 million, but the Tenth Circuit Court of Appeals left Pring with nothing at all.

There was no question that the plaintiff was identifiable as the character. But the court held that the statements were not false representations of fact. In order for a plaintiff to recover, wrote the court, "the story must reasonably be understood as describing actual facts about the plaintiff or her actual conduct. [The story] could [not] reasonably be understood as describing actual facts." The dissenting judge in *Pring* noted that while levitation might be fantasy, fellatio surely was not.

The typical disclaimer that a work is fiction is helpful in cases like this. The fact that the story in *Pring* was labeled humor was used by the court. The court in *Middlebrooks* wrote: "[It] was an obvious work of fiction. It was listed in the fiction section of the Post index, was labeled fiction, and was illustrated with cartoons."

The most recent case resulted in a settlement—thus having no precedential value—after a carload of publicity. In *Anderson v. Avco Embassy Pictures et al.*, Jane Anderson, a Harvard associate professor of clinical psychiatry, sued everyone remotely connected with the film version of *The Bell Jar*, Sylvia Plath's autobiographical novel. Anderson claimed she was identifiable as a character in the movie. Unlike the real-life Anderson, though, the character, the plaintiff claimed, was falsely portrayed as a suicidal lesbian. The case was tried before a Boston jury in January, 1987, and Anderson got a settlement of $150,000.

Fiction and Public Figures

Plaintiffs who are public figures must prove in addition to everything else that the defendant acted with "actual malice," the legal term commonly defined as "knowing falsity or reckless disregard of the truth." (Proving actual malice is important even when the plaintiff isn't a public figure, because that dispenses with the need to prove actual damages.) Other than Bindrim, there appear to be no reported decisions concerning public figures who sued for libel in a work of fiction, and there have been only a handful who sued for invasion of privacy. In Bindrim, the court found actual malice because Davis had been present at the encounter group and knew what the truth was. But no courts have held, as some lawyers worry they might, that because fiction is the opposite of truth, actual malice is a given in a work of fiction.

Indeed, courts have gone the other way. *Hicks v. Casablanca Records* involved the film *Agatha* and the Ballantine paperback tie-in. The story provided a fictional explanation for the English writer Agatha Christie's actual mysterious disappearance at one point in her life, and Christie's heirs sued for violation of their right of privacy. The court stated that because anyone would know the work was fictitious and because the author did not attempt to present the disputed facts as true, there was no "deliberate falsification" of facts, and thus no actual malice and no liability.

Fictionalization that purports to be the truth or close to it, however, is more likely to create problems. In *The Warren Spahn Story*, a nonfiction young adult biography of the baseball star, the author made up dialogue, attributed thoughts and feelings to Spahn that had no basis in reality or in the author's research, and misstated a multitude of facts about "Spahn's childhood, his relationship with his father, the courtship of his wife, important events during their marriage, and his military experience." This, the court held, constituted "material and substantial falsification," or the requisite actual malice, and Spahn won his case. Some older cases, arguably no longer good law, make the same point.

Some lawyers have explained Bindrim's victory by pointing out that Gwen Davis had signed a nondisclosure agreement with the psychologist before she attended his sessions; the court, they maintain, was influenced by that evidence of bad faith. *Bindrim* is an odd case—the only one recently in which a plaintiff has won. But the straining of much of the decisions' reasoning and the language of the dissents in *Springer* and *Pring* suggest that *Bindrim* wasn't entirely a fluke and that authors should take the threat seriously.

Most publishers do, and, since *Bindrim*, have instructed their editors that novels with a factual or autobiographical component are candidates for libel review, and may ask for changes. What should those changes be? As noted above, courts have seized on all manner of arguably transparent disguises—changing physical description, location, profession, age—and these are the changes lawyers suggest. Another possibility is switching a character's gender, if that doesn't mess up the plot. But at best, this is a fingers-crossed area of libel and privacy review.

It also makes sense, when christening a character with an arbitrarily chosen name, to make sure there isn't one listed in the local telephone book, and it is folly in fiction not to include a disclaimer. All of these measures make it more likely a potential plaintiff will be dissuaded by a responsible lawyer from suing, because he or she has only the slimmest chance of winning.

Review/Chapter 4

Plaintiffs who sue authors of fiction for libel or invasion of privacy must prove that:

✔a reasonable person would understand that the fictional character was the plaintiff

✔readers would believe the defamatory material was true

Fiction writers can decrease the chances they'll be sued successfully by:

✔including a disclaimer

✔making sure a fictional character based on a real person is somehow different from the real person, in such factors as age, occupation, place of residence, physical appearance

✔avoiding mixing real names with fictional ones

✔checking telephone directories in the city where the story is set to avoid accidentally using a real person's name

Chapter 5
Pornography and the Serious Writer

Herald Price Fahringer

Sooner or later, almost every writer will need to deal with sexual material in one form or another. How do you make sure that frank or realistic treatments don't cross the line into pornography? It's sometimes a tough call, but this chapter outlines what has been established:
1. Three criteria for obscenity established by the Supreme Court.
2. The protection that's available for serious literary works.
3. How community standards are used in determining what's obscene and how those standards have changed.
4. The different standard used for judging of sexual material involving children.

The law governing the publication and sale of literature that may be deemed legally obscene has not changed much in the past two decades. In 1973 the Supreme Court revised the formula devised for measuring whether a book or film is obscene in the case of *Miller v. California* (1973). For a publication to be found obscene it must be established that:
1. It appeals to the average person's prurient interest in sex;
2. It depicts sexual conduct in a patently offensive way;
3. And, when taken as a whole, it lacks serious literary, artistic, political, or scientific value.

Since then, the law has remained fairly stable. Each branch of this equation is important and must be understood. The "average person" refers to a normal, healthy adult—not a child or someone easily influenced or especially sensitive to certain brands of sexual material, as established in *Pinkus v. United States* (1978).

Community Standards Determine What's Obscene

"Patently offensive" requires that the material substantially exceed contemporary community standards of a set geographical area in which the material is sold or distributed. In many jurisdictions the boundaries of the community are fixed by county lines. However, in some areas like New York and California, a statewide standard is used.

(Federal obscenity prosecutions are established in the United States Code. Virtually every state has an obscenity statute in its penal code. But, since we operate under a federal constitution, those statutes must conform to the standards fixed by the United States Supreme Court.)

"Prurient interest" is defined as a shameful, morbid, or unhealthy interest in sex—not a normal attraction. The Supreme Court has determined that an author's arousal of normal sexual instincts should not be criminal. Therefore, in judging a book, the jury may not consider its effect on the perverse or those persons who harbor ambiguous or unorthodox sexual preferences.

There is one significant exception to this rule. If a book is designed for and primarily disseminated to a clearly defined deviant group, rather than the public at large, it may be found obscene if it appeals to the prurient interest of members of that class, as seen in *Mishkin v. New York* (1966). This means that if an author wrote a book designed to appeal to the prurient interest of homosexuals, it could be found obscene, if its candor went substantially beyond contemporary community standards and it lacked serious literary, artistic, political, or scientific value.

Serious Literary Works Protected

The branch of the Supreme Court's formula governing obscenity that protects most writers is the "serious literary, artistic, political, or scientific value" standard. For a prosecutor to convict an author, he or she must prove beyond a reasonable doubt that the story lacks those designated redeeming values. Recently, the Supreme Court concluded that a book's literary value cannot be judged by general community standards, which would relegate that judgment to a kind of majority rule. Instead the Court held:

The proper inquiry is not whether an ordinary member of any given community would find serious literary, artistic, political or scientific value in an allegedly obscene material, but whether a reasonable person would find such value in the material taken as a whole. (Pope v. Illinois, 1987.)

And, of course, "taken as a whole" means that the book cannot be judged by an isolated passage that may have prurient appeal beyond community standards. The book must be judged in its entirety.

Standards Have Changed

Perhaps the most significant development in this whole area of litigation is the sexual revolution launched by the sixties. Explicit mag-

azines such as *Playboy*, *Penthouse*, and *Hustler*, with their
gynecological photography, confront us everywhere we look—on
newsstands, in drugstores, and at airport terminals. The advent of
cable television and VCRs has brought explicit sex into every
person's living room. This form of saturation has rendered the sexual
candor of such works as *Lady Chatterley's Lover*, *The Tropic of Can-
cer*, and *The Memoirs of a Woman of Pleasure* (which at one time
were the subject of strenuous obscenity prosecutions) obsolete.

In light of these developments, prosecutors in most major cities
have concentrated on materials that deal with the most gruesome
forms of bizarre sex—such as child pornography, bestiality, or sado-
masochism. And even in those cases, with the exception of child pornography, the film or book, to be successfully prosecuted, must
present these sexual subjects without any artistic gloss. There is every indication that this trend will continue unabated and in that circumstance lies the safety of serious authors.

Child Pornography

A very special problem created for authors, however, lies in the
field of children and sex. In 1982, the Supreme Court sustained a
New York statute that made it a felony for a person to produce any
play, film, or illustrated book containing sexual conduct by a child
less than sixteen years old or the lewd display of his or her genitals.
Conspicuously missing from this law was the protective language requiring that the book appeal to the reader's prurient interest, exceed
contemporary community standards, and lack literary or artistic
value.

Ardent patriots of the First Amendment argued that this statute
could be applied to illustrated books concerned with sexual education of children and to Margaret Mead's *Coming of Age in Samoa*.
However, the Court expressed its expectation that state prosecutors
would never apply the statute to such worthwhile materials because,
in that circumstance, it might well implicate serious constitutional
consequences, *Ferber v. New York* (1982). If an author wrote an illustrated book on pedophilia, it is possible the book might be the subject of an official investigation in some communities.

Today almost every state has some form of a child pornography
statute similar to that of New York. The federal provisions governing
the sexual exploitation of children are gathered under Title 18 of the
United States Code.

There are those who mistakenly believed that the written word, no
matter how sexually frank, fell within the protective sweep of the
First Amendment. That premise was argued in the case of *Kaplan v.
California* (1973), and was rejected by the Supreme Court. The Court
concluded that even the written word, without illustration, enjoys no
absolute protection under the First Amendment.

In closing, there are scholars and jurists who are convinced that the concept of obscenity cannot be defined with sufficient specificity to provide adequate notice to persons who create and distribute materials dealing with sexual subjects. Certainly, the Supreme Court's struggle with this issue has led to a sad succession of decisions that has left the issue of obscenity hopelessly muddled. Both in letter and in spirit, these obscenity cases have entangled states in ambiguous moral and constitutional questions leading to utter confusion in this area of the law. But, despite this lack of certainty in the law, authors who write seriously on the subject of sex have little to fear.

Review/Chapter 5

For a publication to be found obscene, it must:
　✔appeal to the average person's prurient interest in sex
　✔depict sexual conduct in a way that is patently offensive
　✔lack serious literary, artistic, political, or scientific value
These criteria have been defined more fully:
　✔an "average person" is a normal, healthy adult and "prurient interest" is shameful, morbid or unhealthy interest in sex
　✔material that is patently offensive must exceed contemporary community standards
　✔a work's literary or scientific value must be judged when looking at the work as a whole

Chapter 6
Photography and the Law

Richard H. Logan III

Writers deal with photography two ways: First, some writers take photographs to accompany their stories, and must know what they can photograph. Second, most writers work with photographers and photographs, helping decide what photos will be used with their stories and perhaps writing captions. Either way, you need to understand:

1. When you need to get the subject's written permission before publishing a photograph.

2. How to avoid being charged with libel or obscenity resulting from the use of photographs.

3. What kinds of insurance you should carry, whether you're a full-time photographer or a writer who takes pictures.

4. How to deal with the military, courts, and other authorities who want to control your actions.

5. Hints for running your own photography business, including pricing and ethical guidelines.

After the press photographer has been taking photographs for some time, he or she will probably take a picture that someone wishes to use in an advertisement. If it is a picture of a store front, building, or some other object with no recognizable human beings shown, there is ordinarily no legal problem. The photographer can sell or give the picture to the client who wants to use it in an ad and no one is likely to be involved in a legal suit. If the person is the recognizable store proprietor or some member of the family, use of the photo in an ad carries with it the implication that the owner had consented to the publication of the photograph.

Getting Permission from Subjects

If the subject of the picture is another person, however, even a model or a good friend, the photographer should obtain a written model release before using any picture for other than ordinary news purposes. State laws vary, but it is always safer to get a signed model release than to rely on oral consent. Even the written consent of a minor to the use of a picture is not adequate, for the signature of the parent or guardian is necessary to make the model release valid. In most states, a minor is any person under the age of eighteen. A few states still retain twenty-one as the age of majority, and in some states the age is nineteen.

The more exact the language and the broader the release, the greater the legal protection given to the photographer. But even a written model release does not prevent the photographer from being sued if the picture has been altered or used in some way embarrassing to the subject for which the model has not given legal consent. It is also important to remember that the release must be voluntary and not obtained by coercion or fraud.

From experience, I have found it best to obtain a model release at the time the picture is taken. In my release, I usually mention a consideration, which may be a sum of money, the gift of a finished photograph, or something else of value. I also include the date and point out that the person signing the release consents to various advertising and publication uses, including the electronic media. Photographers can usually buy model release blanks from firms advertising in photography journals, or they may have their own forms printed or typed.

The Subject's Right of Privacy

The model release comes under the right of privacy. There have been legal cases involving the right of privacy in which the photograph in question was not published but was only seen by a third person. Public figures, generally speaking, have little or no right of privacy, and the person who takes a picture of an actor, famous scientist, or politician has the right to reproduce it in publications for informative purposes. It cannot, however, be used for advertising under any circumstances without the subject's permission.

The majority of lawsuits brought against photographers involve the right of privacy. As with most legal rulings, what constitutes an offense in this area depends on the laws of a particular state and the intent of the photographer. In New York, photographers can display samples of their work in their studio but must remove any picture for which they do not have consent if the subject of the picture objects. Other states may or may not allow such display; therefore, it's best to be familiar with your own state laws.

If a picture is taken in pursuit of news and published in a newspaper or magazine, the courts have usually held that the same picture

Photography and the Law ∞ 49

A Sample Model Release

For value received, the receipt and adequacy of which are hereby acknowledged, I hereby give (name of firm or publication) the absoute right and permission to copyright and/or publish, and/or resell photographic portraits or pictures of me, or in which I may be included in whole or in part, for art, advertising, trade, or any other lawful purpose whatsoever.

I hereby waive any right that I may have to inspect and/or approve the finished product or the advertising copy that may be used in connection therewith, or the use to which it may be applied.

I hereby release, discharge, and agree to save (name of firm or publication) harmless from any liability by virtue of any blurring, distortion, alteration, optical illusion, or use in composite form, whether intentional or otherwise, that may occur or be produced in the making of said pictures, or in any processing tending toward the completion of the finished product.

Date_____ Model_____

                              Address_____

                              _____

Witness_____

may be used without the subject's consent in an ad to increase circulation of the publication or in some similar way. The picture cannot be used in connection with a product, however, or any other item not related to the original legitimate news in the publication. The same rule usually applies to the use of a news picture in a book if the picture is of an informative nature or if it is of a public figure who, in a sense, has more or less surrendered the greater part of the right of privacy in becoming a public figure.

There are also questions of decency to consider in the taking of photographs. If the photographer is in doubt about a picture, it is best to ask the editor or some equally well-informed person, such as the newspaper's attorney, for advice.

Libel and Truth

In the Roaring Twenties, from 1924 to 1932, the New York *Evening Graphic* became famous for its sensational journalism and clever photomontage reproductions called *composographs.* In a circulation war with other New York newspapers, the *Graphic* used these photographs as a means of attracting a great number of readers. The composographs were made by superimposing models onto real photographs or by cutting out people's heads and placing them on the bodies of models posed in such a way as to illustrate news stories in the paper.

Even though there were no photographic wire services at the time of Lindbergh's safe arrival in Paris, the *Graphic* came out with a "scoop" in the form of a composograph showing Charles Lindbergh in Paris after the first nonstop solo flight across the Atlantic. Many people knew the picture was not real, but they bought the paper anyway. The captions stated that the pictures were composographs. Such pictures would not be published today because of a change in newspaper ethics and in the laws of libel and privacy.

Because truth is one of the defenses in libel cases and photographs are considered to be actual representations of scenes, it would appear that libel suits from "true" photographs would never develop. This is not necessarily so, although such suits are uncommon. Libel suits have been won where the photograph subjected a person to ridicule or was otherwise degrading. Photographs may not always tell the truth because of the perspective that certain lenses create. The distortion may make the subject appear grotesque or even obscene.

Libel cases may also derive from the captions on photographs, from improper use of photographs, or even from cases of mistaken identity. Many libel suits involving photographs come not from the caption but from the use of the photograph with an article that may imply that the subject is dishonest when that is not so or in some other way debases the subject's character.

Generally speaking, news pictures reporting current happenings or illustrating other news items of public interest need not have the permission of the subject in order to be used. Persons who attend public events may have their picture taken as part of the audience, even though they may not desire that this be done. One person in such a situation cannot be singled out, however, unless he or she is newsworthy. Here, the fine line between what is newsworthy and what is not may be difficult to determine at times. The photographer is usually safe in taking such a picture if it is customary to do so at certain types of events, such as a New Year's Eve celebration, a fashion show, or a political rally.

Obscenity

Determining the difference between an obscene and an artistic picture in photographing nudes is somewhat difficult, particularly in the light of many court decisions that have obscured the meaning of obscenity. In the more recent court cases there are at least four factors which must be dealt with: (1) whether the viewers are adults or children; (2) whether the photograph is in the form of movies or stills; (3) whether the photographic material is considered hard-core pornography, rather than artistic; and (4) whether the use of the United States Postal Service is involved.

Because of a number of liberal court interpretations of the First and Fourteenth Amendments of the United States Constitution dealing with free speech and a free press, there is very little left under federal and most state laws which can be considered "obscene," except in some cases of sexual activity being pictured. What is permissible in motion pictures may not be permissible in single still photos, or a series of still photos depicting the same material that appeared in the motion picture. Children often come under more restrictive laws than do adults.

Determining just what is hard-core pornography will vary from one legal decision to another, and even though the photographs are offensive, distasteful, or lewd, they may not be considered legally obscene. The line of demarcation can be very close in a court decision, even depending upon the publisher's intent and the advertising. The term "hard-core pornography" itself raises doubts, because it is legally imprecise in nature. State laws on obscenity and hard-core pornography will vary, even within the federal court interpretation.

The United States Postal Service has substantially changed (as a result of certain legal decisions) its former policy on "questionable photographs," although the present policies are not as liberal as might be expected. Even though the showing of pubic hair, or those photos which were thought to incite immoral thoughts or deeds are no longer necessarily on the prohibition list, those items that do fall within hard-core pornography or depict sexual activity may be prohibited. There have always been exceptions to post office policies when photographic material is for medical or similar purposes. If you are in doubt, consult your local postmaster or other postal authority for the latest information.

Copyrighting Photographs

If you wish to prevent unauthorized use of a picture, you should make sure "© [your name]" is printed alongside each photo. You can also register your claim for a copyright with the Register of Copyrights, Library of Congress, Washington, DC 20559. The cost of each copyright is $10, and two copies of each photograph must be sent for deposit with the application. Application forms may be obtained from that office.

Because copyrighting each photograph is expensive, some photographers have placed a number of individual photographs on a piece of photographic paper and registered the whole group for one fee. In the case of photographs being published in the editorial sections of a magazine, the publisher may copyright the magazine and thus protect the photograph, provided the photographer has retained the right to resell the picture. Every time the picture is published, the words "Copyright by . . ." and the owner's name should appear either on the published picture or just below it, unless the whole publication is copyrighted. The copyright symbol, ©, accompanied by the copyright owner's name, is frequently used. The date need not appear on photographs.

If publication of the picture is permitted without the copyright notice either on it or with it, the owner loses copyright protection. In general, for photographs published after January 1, 1978, the copyright is good for the life of the photographer plus fifty years. The photographer need not apply immediately for a copyright; it may be obtained within three months after first publication. The notice of copyright must appear with all photographs whether the copyright has been registered or not, if the photographer wishes to protect the photo.

One publishing firm I know published a children's book for an author with the copyright notice inadvertently omitted. The author later wanted to protect herself by copyright but could not do so because the book had been published first without the notice of copyright. Under the law there are some means of recovery when a copyright notice has been omitted or printed in error. Contact the Copyright Office, Library of Congress, Washington, DC 20559 for details.

Insurance

Because camera equipment is quite expensive and subject to theft, breakage, falling off a pier into the water, and many other hazards, the cheapest investment a photographer can make is insurance on equipment. The policy with the greatest coverage is called a *floater policy*, which covers almost anything that can happen to the photographer's equipment outside of mechanical repairs or deterioration from normal use. I have found some insurance agents unfamiliar with this type of policy, so it is advisable to be sure that the agent understands your needs.

A second type of policy covers fire, theft, and storm damage but not breakage from accidental dropping and is included in the insurance of either a person's place of business or household effects. Different companies have different types of policies, and it is necessary to make comparisons among various coverage plans offered before making a decision. Premiums for floater policies normally run about $2.50 per $100 valuation, with the premium for household policies usually less. If the photographer has only a small amount of photo equipment, it would perhaps be better to insure it under the latter type of policy. If he or she has a considerable amount of equipment, however, carries it around frequently, and uses it in earning either all or part of his or her income, the floater policy is perhaps more advantageous because of the wide protection it affords. Generally speaking, there is a minimum premium of about $21 per year on a floater policy.

As a photographer, you should also protect yourself from financial loss brought on by suits or out-of-court settlements with subjects injured from a fall or similar accident while working with you or while on your property.

All sorts of freak accidents occur, injuring and sometimes killing persons. One such accident killed a high school cheerleader while she was posing with six other cheerleaders on a crossbar of the goalpost. It was the last picture of a shooting session, and the students were perched on the crossbar about ten feet above the ground, when the bar broke and one of the goalposts fell on the girl, fatally injuring her.

Normally, a photographer working for a company will be protected by the company's personal liability insurance, but a self-employed photographer will need his or her own protection. Even though the photographer may not in any way be at fault in an accident, lawsuits are costly and no one knows how a jury will decide. Personal liability insurance coverage should be discussed with several agents and the cost and protection compared for the various policies.

The photographer who has employees who handle money should consider bonding those employees through an insurance company. Most large companies follow this procedure, because it is impossible to determine who is honest or dishonest until the person embezzles or otherwise misappropriates the funds or property of the firm.

The most trusted person in the firm often turns to embezzling, because of that very trust. In bank embezzlements the guilty party is often the trusted "little old lady" who has been an employee for many years and is well thought of in the community. Or the embezzler may be the accountant or financial officer who is a church member and an apparently outstanding citizen of the community, until it is discovered that he or she has "borrowed" company funds to place bets on horse races or to invest in highly speculative securities. The embezzler always had every intention of paying back the funds, of course, but was unable to do so because of losses. Remember that many small businesses have been bankrupted by an employee's dis-

honest actions. Bonding insurance is reasonable in cost and is sold
by a great number of insurance companies.

Dealing with Military, Police, and Courts

Many newsworthy pictures are obtained through the cooperation of
police, fire, a   military authorities. The photographer covering such
beats will soon learn what pictures are permitted and how to get
along with civilian and military authorities without becoming med-
dlesome. In large cities, press photographers carry special passes
from local officials that allow them to go into places where there are
fires, accidents, or other tragedies closed to the general public.

There have been occasions when even the police have destroyed a
photographer's film or camera or roughed the photographer up per-
sonally in some way. These cases are rare, and usually the photographer from a publication or press organization receives favorable
treatment from the authorities.

Military authorities have more restrictions on taking pictures, and
sometimes it is difficult to get pictures of a crash of a plane, an ex-
plosion on a base, or some other restricted area. Often the military
will release only pictures that their own photographers have taken
and will not allow the news photographers to take pictures on their
own.

Various agencies of the federal government have a "managed news"
policy and will not allow certain types of pictures to be taken or
statements quoted from government officials. This policy varies,
sometimes being quite lenient and other times, quite strict.

When an accident involves two of the city's fire trucks or a police
officer wrecks a car while under the influence of alcohol, a photographer will usually find it extremely difficult to get pictures of the
event. The agency in question may pass it off as "taking all measures
to protect the city and the public at large" or some similar excuse.

Whether pictures can be taken in a courtroom depends largely on
the judge and the custom of that particular court. The American Bar
Association in 1937 adopted a rule known as "Canon 35," which
stated that the association felt that taking pictures while the court
was in session or during recesses detracted from the dignity of the
court and otherwise created misconceptions in the mind of the public and that any type of photography in the courtroom should be
prohibited. The National Press Photographers' Association fought
hard to have this rule changed, using as a basis for argument the
fact that cameras with fast lenses and high-speed film could take pictures in the courtroom without distracting or interfering with court
proceedings.

An amendment in 1952 provided that certain proceedings could be
photographed. Actually, the *Canons of Judicial Ethics* are not laws
but guidelines for the nation's judges and attorneys. Some states

strongly enforce this rule, and a violation can lead to a contempt citation with a possible fine or jail sentence for the photographer.

Pretrial Publicity

In June 1966, the U.S. Supreme Court ruled that Dr. Samuel Sheppard, Cleveland, Ohio, had not had a fair trial when convicted of his wife's murder in 1954. The decision of the court was based on the widespread coverage by radio, TV, and newspapers of Dr. Sheppard's arrest and trial. The Court held that because of the nature and intensity of this coverage, Dr. Sheppard was entitled to a new trial.

A number of other cases have developed in the same area, all having to do with pretrial news coverage. Because of such cases, news media are finding it increasingly difficult to hold interviews, take photographs, and write news stories on important criminal cases.

Running Your Own Business

A photographer employed by a publication does not need an occupation license. When you go into business for yourself, you will be governed by the laws and ordinances governing businesses of the community in which you live and/or work. There are certain restrictions covering sanitation, commercial zoning, sales tax licenses, occupation licenses, and other areas a professional photographer must observe. It is wise to inquire what regulations affect photographers before establishing a part-time or full-time business. Some cities permit darkrooms in residential areas but not studios. Others may permit home studios but restrict advertising and displays or even have regulations on customer parking. These restrictions will vary from area to area. By joining one of the professional photographer's associations, you can often learn more quickly about new legal and ethical problems. Of course, you also have the opportunity to attend clinics and conferences and to meet other persons active in the field.

Ethics in Photography

Ethics is one important aspect of photography that the beginner might never consider. An ethical violation might not be brought before a court of law, although lawsuits can arise from such infringements, but both the photographer's business and personal reputation can be damaged by an inadvertent action if he or she is unaware of ethical complications that may arise. Photography has its own special pitfalls, and they are not always easy to predict or judge with mere common sense and good instincts.

The photographer seldom, if ever, needs to come into direct physical contact with a subject, and it is best to refrain from touching the person in any way, especially in taking studio pictures or portraits. Although a young child may be lifted or moved about slightly, young people and adults should be directed either by voice or by gesture or both, without actual physical contact.

The photographer who wants to have a good reputation should use discretion when alone in the studio with a subject. For example, when I once owned a portrait studio in a small city, a young lady telephoned to ask if I took drape shots. I replied that I did but had no one in the studio and that she should bring her mother, sister, or a girl friend to help her with the drape. I prefer to have a woman assistant to smooth the wrinkles from a dress, straighten sleeves, put hair in place, or otherwise arrange a subject's clothes and help with posing. Even though the photographer may innocently touch someone, the subject may receive the wrong impression due to the reputation that fiction has given photographers.

The photographer should never give the picture of a subject to anyone else without the subject's express permission, even though the picture may have been used for a news story and permission may have been obtained when the picture was taken. A boy may come in and ask for a photograph of a pretty girl, claiming to be her boyfriend. The girl may not want him to have her picture, and although giving him the picture without her consent might not bring about a lawsuit, it could very well damage the photographer's public image permanently.

Photographers need to build their reputation on sound ethical and business practices. False advertising, shoddy work, or other unethical tactics have no place in the professional photographer's life. The Professional Photographers of America, Inc., and other similar organizations have adopted codes of ethics, and it is a good idea for beginning photographers to familiarize themselves with these codes as a guide to their professional conduct.

Good Taste
Gruesome pictures of tragedies are taken from time to time. For example, a Buddhist nun is photographed after setting herself on fire, the burning funeral pyre of a great leader such as Mahatma Gandhi is shown, or grisly pictures of accident victims are made. Newspaper readers often criticize the publication of pictures that they think are in poor taste or are unpleasant to view.

Much of the decision as to whether to publish such a picture in the paper rests upon the editor. Photographers working with newspapers or wire services will know what to take and what to omit from experience and from guidelines set down by the organization's policy. Although there may be some legal questions involved in such pictures, usually the publication of gory or distasteful photos comes under the category of ethics rather than of legality. Such pictures do serve as warnings to others and definitely fall into the newsworthy class; however, some papers thrive on sensationalism and carry the publication of such pictures much too far. The paper should keep in mind the dignity of the victims of the tragedy, as well as the feelings of the audience. Whether to publish a picture of a tragedy is often a difficult decision for the photo editor to make.

Pricing

Two of the greatest mistakes beginning photographers make are that they tend to price their work too cheaply and they attempt freelance assignments for which they are not qualified.

The photographer should charge enough money to absorb the costs not only of materials but also of time, car expenses, depreciation on equipment, and other overhead expenses, such as insurance and taxes. Even the beginning photographer should charge two or three times as much for an 8x10 photograph as the customer would pay to have his or her own negative enlarged to an 8x10 size at the drugstore.

Beginning photographers should charge less, in most cases, for their work than a professional because they lack skill. They should not, however, try to take business away from professionals by pricing their work ridiculously low. Doing so not only reflects on the photographer's character but hurts the entire photographic profession as well.

I have had unethical and mostly inexperienced photographers solicit some of my better accounts by offering to make photographs for about one fourth my regular prices. Many times the account would tell me about such photographers, remarking that the other photographer was not even considered because the account manager knew that good photographs could not be obtained at the price quoted.

Once, when I had my own industrial photography business in Denver, I was asked to quote a price for taking a number of 8x10 photographs of the interior of a very famous bar. I went to the establishment and talked to the owner, and we came to an agreement of $10 for each 8x10 glossy photograph, a price somewhat lower than I normally charged. When I went back to make a definite appointment to take the pictures, the owner told me that he had changed his mind because an airman from one of the nearby bases had offered to do the job for 35¢ per 8x10 photograph. As a result, neither of us got the job. The owner felt that I must be overcharging him at $10 a picture, and he did not hire the airman because he did not believe he could do the work properly.

Review/Chapter 6

A photographer should obtain a written model release from a subject if the photo is to be used for anything other than ordinary news purposes. Most forms contain:

✔mention of a consideration, such as a copy of the photo
✔permission to use the photograph for art, advertising, and trade
✔permission to use the photograph in any medium
✔a release of liability for distortion, blurring, and other alterations
✔blanks for the subject's name and address and the date

Four factors to consider in dealing with potentially obscene photographs are whether:
✔the photography is still or movie film
✔the viewers will be adults or children
✔the material could be considered hard-core, rather than artistic
✔the material will be sent through the U.S. Postal Service

Every time a photograph is published, it should be accompanied by a copyright notice. The notice should include:
✔the words "Copyright by" or the symbol ©
✔the owner's name

Photographers may need several types of insurance, including:
✔coverage of camera equipment
✔personal liability protection in case a subject is injured while working with the photographer
✔bonding for employees who handle large amounts of money

Good ethical practices for photographers include:
✔using voice or gesture to direct subjects, not physical contact
✔never giving photographs to anyone other than the subject without permission
✔considering the dignity of the victims and the feelings of the audience before publishing photos of tragedies

Chapter 7
Ten Questions About Copyright

Victor W. Marton

Nobody likes to think about copyright, but nobody likes to have their work stolen or misused. This chapter will give you the basics about copyright law without weighing you down with too many technicalities. It covers:

1. How the revised law that went into effect January 1, 1978 compares to the old law.

2. How to protect your copyright on material that's published in a magazine.

3. What to do if your work is published without a copyright notice.

4. Why you don't have to file a copyright application with the Copyright Office to be protected.

5. How to know when you need permission to use excerpts from another author's work.

6. Guidelines for using copyrighted materials on public radio or TV broadcasts.

1. First of all, what is a copyright?

It is the right, accorded by law, to prohibit the unauthorized copying of original works of literature, art, music, sound recordings, and other creative works of authorship. Also it is the right to prohibit certain other acts that have been likened, by statute or court decisions, to copying. It is the right of the author (that is, the creator of the work) or of someone who has derived that right from the author. A copyright is a form of personal property which is intangible in nature and therefore separate from the property right in any of the physical objects in which the work may be embodied. For example, you would normally own a letter mailed to you by a friend, but the literary property in that letter would ordinarily still be owned by the letter writer.

The copyright statutes of the United States are based on a provision of the U.S. Constitution which provides that "Congress shall have the Power . . . To promote the Progress of Science and useful

Arts, by securing for limited Times to Authors and Inventors the exclusive Right to their respective Writings and Discoveries." And, indeed, there has been such a statute since 1790, when the Second Session of the First Congress passed the first Federal Copyright Law. The present law, which took full effect January 1, 1978, is codified as Title 17 of the United States Code. On March 1, 1989, the United States joined the Berne Convention for the Protection of Literary and Artistic Works. Also on March 1, 1989, amendments to the copyright law that satisfy U.S. treaty obligations under the Convention took effect.

2. What are some of the major provisions of the revised copyright law?

A. Instead of the previous "dual system" of protecting works by common law prior to their publication and under the federal statute after publication, the revised law provides for a single national system of statutory coverage for all copyrightable works, whether they are published or unpublished. For those works already created and under statutory copyright protection as of December 31, 1977, the revised law keeps the first term of twenty-eight years measured from the date of publication, or from the date of registration if registered in the Copyright Office in unpublished form. (Under the old law only certain works such as plays, TV scripts, musical compositions, and lectures could be registered in unpublished form.) The revised law also retains for such works the requirement of renewal in order to have a second term, but it increases the length of the second term from twenty-eight years to forty-seven years so that the total protection possible for these works is seventy-five years. Hence, it is necessary to renew the copyright in works that were in their first term of statutory protection when the revised law took effect on January 1, 1978, in order to have protection beyond the first twenty-eight-year term. Thus, for example, if a work was first published and copyrighted in 1962, a renewal registration for that work must be made in the Copyright Office between December 31, 1989, and December 31, 1990, in order for the copyright protection to subsist beyond December 31, 1990. That renewal would protect it until the year 2037.

B. For a work created on or after January 1, 1978, the revised law specifies that the copyright will subsist from the creation of the work and will endure "for a term consisting of the life of the author and fifty years after his death." In the case of an anonymous work, a pseudonymous work, or a work made for hire, the copyright will generally last "for a term of seventy-five years from the year of its first publication, or a term of one hundred years from the year of its creation, whichever expires first."

C. For works created before January 1, 1978, and still under the common-law protection when the revised law took effect, the term will be that described in paragraph B, but in no case "shall the term of copyright in such a work expire before December 31, 2002; and, if the work is published on or before December 31, 2002, the term of copyright shall not expire before December 31, 2027."

D. Other important provisions of the revised act deal with fair use, sound recordings, U.S. government works, and the compulsory licensing of certain uses of copyright works such as cable antenna television (CATV) and jukeboxes. "Publications on Copyright," a list of circulars and other works on copyright, is available from the Copyright Office, Library of Congress, Washington, DC 20559.

3. How can I protect the ideas in my manuscript from being taken by another writer or an editor and used without paying me?

Ideas are not subject to copyright protection. Copyright protection extends only to literary or pictorial expression chosen by the author to describe, illustrate, or explain an idea. Copyright exists from the moment of creation of an eligible work.

When circulating copies to publishers, producers, or friends, include a copyright notice on the copies. The notice should consist of the word "Copyright" or the symbol c in a circle, the name of the owner of the copyright, and the year date. The use of the notice is the responsibility of the copyright owner and does not require advance permission from, or registration with, the Copyright Office.

4. When I register my literary works in unpublished form, will I have to pay a registration fee for each work, or can I register a collection and pay only one fee?

A collection of unpublished works by the same author—such as a collection of poems—may be registered on a single application form with the $10 filing fee, if the collection bears a single title, for example "Poems of Jane Doe 1990." A collection of works published within a twelve month period by the same author—such as a collection of published newspaper columns—may be registered on a single application form accompanied by a form GR/CP and the $10 filing fee. Contact the Copyright Office for additional information on registration of collections.

5. Will publication of a literary work without a notice of copyright cause loss of copyright, as it did under the former law?

Prior to January 1, 1978, publication without a notice of copyright resulted in the loss of copyright protection. Between January 1, 1978 and February 28, 1989, publication of a "relatively small number of copies" without a notice of copyright did not cause loss of copyright protection, but the work would lose protection if no effort was made to correct the error and if the work was not registered within five years of publication. Mandatory notice of copyright has been abolished for works published for the first time on or after March 1, 1989. Failure to place a notice of copyright on copies or phonorecords of such works can no longer result in the loss of copyright.

6. If my article, poem, or story is to be published in a magazine, how does the revised law affect my rights?

A. The revised law provides that the transfer of the ownership of a copyright, or of the ownership of any exclusive right comprised in a copyright, must generally be in writing and signed by the owner of the right conveyed. Thus, ordinarily only nonexclusive rights are transferable orally.

B. Also, the law states that copyright in each separate contribution to a collective work (such as a magazine) is distinct from copyright in the collective work as a whole, and vests initially in the author of the contribution. In the absence of an express transfer of the copyright or of any rights under it, the owner of copyright in the collective work is presumed to have acquired only the privilege of reproducing and distributing the contribution as part of that particular collective work, any revision of that collective work, and any later collective work in the same series.

(Under the language of this clause a publishing company could reprint a contribution from one issue in a later issue of its magazine and could reprint an article from a 1980 edition of an encyclopedia in a 1990 revision of it; the publisher could not revise the contribution itself or include it in a new anthology or an entirely different magazine or other collective work.)

C. Where the author retains the copyright in a contribution to a magazine, the author may make it a requirement that, as a condition of his authorization of public distribution of copies, the contribution bear a separate notice of copyright in the author's name.

D. Prior to March 1, 1989, a single notice of copyright applicable to the magazine as a whole was generally sufficient to satisfy the notice provisions of the law with respect to separate contributions, regardless of the ownership of copyright in the contributions and whether or not they were previously published. For works published on or after March 1, 1989, the law provides that a single notice covering the collective work as a whole can defeat a defense of "innocent infringement."

E. Prior to March 1, 1989, if the person named in a single notice applicable to a collective work as a whole is not the owner of copyright in a separate contribution that does not bear its own notice, the error may be remedied in accordance with the special provisions to be found in Chapter 4 of the revised act. If for any reason a writer should submit material to an uncopyrighted publication, he or she may request that the editor show the author's personal copyright notice (Copyright, the year, author's name) on the first page of the story or article, or alongside the poem.

7. With a term of life plus fifty years and no renewal, how can I retrieve a copyright on a work that I may have signed away?

The revised law eliminates the renewal provision except for works that are already in their first term of statutory protection on January 1, 1978. Instead, for transfer of rights made by an author or certain of the author's heirs after January 1, 1978, the revised act generally permits the author or certain heirs to terminate the transfer after thirty-five years, by serving written notice on the transferee within specified time limits.

For works already under statutory copyright protection when the revised law took effect, a similar right of termination is provided with respect to transfers covering the newly added years extending the present maximum term of the copyright from fifty-six to seventy-five years. Within certain time limits, an author or specified heirs of the author are generally entitled to file a notice terminating the author's transfers covering any part of the period that has now been added to the end of the second term of copyright, in a work already under statutory protection on January 1, 1978.

8. With a life plus fifty term of copyright, when does a copyright expire on a work by two authors, one of whom dies twenty years before the other?

With regard to a work which is subject to the life plus fifty term and which is a joint work by two or more authors, the term will consist of "the life of the last surviving author and fifty years after such last surviving author's death." A "joint work" is defined in the revised act as a work prepared by two or more authors "with the intention that their contributions be merged into inseparable or interdependent parts of a unitary whole."

9. How important is it for me to register my work and pay the $10 fee?

The law establishes your ownership to the copyright as soon as you create a work. Just type Copyright, the year, and your name on the first page of the manuscript. It's not necessary to formally register it with the Copyright Office unless you anticipate that you will have to either (a) challenge someone who is infringing your work or (b) defend yourself against a suit for infringement by someone else who claims your work copies his or hers. Registration is a prerequisite to any suit for infringement.

10. How do I know how much I can use of copyrighted material without having to ask permission of the owner?

Although the revised law does not provide any rule of thumb, it does specify that, notwithstanding the rights granted to the copyright owner, the *fair use* of a copyrighted work, including such use by reproduction in copies or phonorecords or by any other specified means, for purposes such as criticism, comment, news reporting, teaching (including multiple copies for classroom use), scholarship, or research, is *not* an infringement of copyright. In determining whether the use made of a work in any particular instance is fair use, the factors to be considered shall include:

A. the purpose and character of the use, including whether such use is of a commercial nature or is for nonprofit educational purposes;

B. the nature of the copyrighted work;

C. the amount and substantiality of the portion used in relation to the copyrighted work as a whole; and

D. the effect of the use upon the potential market for or value of the copyrighted work.

Editorial Note: *If you wish to receive materials on the revised law that the Copyright Office issues from time to time, the office will be glad to put you on its mailing list. Write: The Copyright Office, Library of Congress, Washington, DC 20559 with your request and be sure to give your full name, address, and ZIP code.*

Copyright Guidelines Available

Writers and educators who would like to know the guidelines on photocopying (without copyright infringement) that have been issued by both publishers and librarians can get copies from the respective professional associations:

Photocopying by Academic, Public and Non-profit Research Libraries, a guide to legitimate photocopying of copyrighted materials, is available for $2 prepaid, to the Association of American Publishers, 2005 Massachusetts Ave. NW, Washington DC 20036.

Librarians Guide to the New Copyright Law is available for $4 prepaid to the American Library Association, Order Department, 50 East Huron Street, Chicago, IL 60611.

Writers who are concerned with either creating for public radio or TV or using material broadcast by these stations should refer to the following chart published in *Public Telecommunications Review* of the National Association of Educational Broadcasters which offers some guidelines. (In the chart, "SCA" refers to an industry term for radio subcarrier authorization—a subchannel available to most FM broadcasters. Receivable only through special converters, its most common noncommercial use is the broadcasting of special programming to the visually handicapped. Its most common commercial use is broadcast recordings such as Muzak.)

Review/Chapter 7

Two major changes under the revised copyright law are:
✔published and unpublished works are equally protected
✔the term of copyright is now the life of the author plus fifty years
A notice of copyright should be included on the first page of a manuscript before it is circulated to anyone else. The notice should include:
✔the words "Copyright by" or the symbol c in a circle
✔the year
✔the author's name
Copyright exists as soon as you create a work, so it's not necessary to register the work unless you anticipate that you will have to either:
✔challenge someone who uses your work without permission
✔defend yourself against someone who claims your work copies his or hers
Factors that determine whether the use of someone's work without that person's permission qualifies as "fair use" include:
✔the purpose of the use, including whether it's commercial or educational
✔the amount of the work that's used in relation to the work as a whole
✔the effect on the value of the original work

More about Copyright and Rights

Since 1978 when the new Copyright Law went into effect, your copyright exists as soon as you create a work. All you need do is type the words Copyright 1990 (or whatever year you create the work) and your name on the first page of your manuscript. If you're submitting to foreign markets—say an English language magazine published in Australia—it would be a good idea to use the small letter "c" in a circle rather than the word Copyright since the c-in-a-circle is the international copyright symbol.

Your copyright entitles you to all rights to the manuscript—the power to control that work's reproduction, distribution and adaptation to other forms. In the case of a story, poem or article, the law assumes you are basically selling one time rights to that work to a magazine unless you agree otherwise in writing with the publisher. Some magazines buy "all rights," so if you think you might later want to adapt your story into a play, or turn your article into a nonfiction book, or collect your poems into an anthology, it's not in your best interest to sell all rights to your manuscript.

If you're selling to an American or Canadian magazine, it's best to just sell First North American Serial Rights so that you can retain all other rights for yourself. If you're reselling a manuscript to which you have already sold first rights, then you would offer "Reprint Rights." You would type whatever rights you're offering in the upper right hand corner of your manuscript. Your copyright credit line could be typed right under that.

If you're making a simultaneous submission to any of those magazines in *Writer's Market*® or *Novel and Short Story Writer's Market* which accept same, you could type "Simultaneous submission to non-competing publication at your usual rate," in the upper right hand corner of your manuscript above your copyright credit line.

Answers to Some Frequent Questions about Copyright

How Much Can I Quote?

Q. *How much can I quote from copyrighted materials without infringing on copyright?*

A. There aren't any set number of lines you can quote without getting permission. In determining whether an author has made "fair use" of, or infringed, another's copyrighted work, the copyright law says the factors to be considered shall include: (1) the purpose and character of the use, including whether such use is of a commercial nature or is for nonprofit educational purpose; (2) the nature of the copyrighted work; (3) the amount and substantiality of the portion used in relation to the copyrighted work as a whole; and (4) the effect of the use upon the potential market for or value of the copyrighted work. As current and future legal cases illustrate these points, writers will have a better idea of how these guidelines will be interpreted.

Copyright Procedure

Q. *Is it necessary to register a copyright?*

A. Only if you think you might have to go to court and fight to prove your ownership of the work, is it necessary to register the material with the U.S. Copyright Office. For the proper forms and more information, write to the U.S. Copyright Office, Library of Congress, Washington DC 20559.

Omission of Copyright Notice

Q. *If a publisher inadvertently omits the writer's copyright notice, is the work then placed in the public domain?*

A. Not since March 1, 1989, when the U.S. joined the world-wide Berne Copyright Convention, which does not require a copyright notice. But it's still important to show the copyright notice on all printed material or manuscripts to avoid innocent infringement.

Let Publisher Have Copyright?

Q. *A publisher for whom I am writing an article offers the option of either giving the writer copyright for the piece or keeping it himself. Is it possible that the publisher could do a better job of handling copyright and legal matters stemming from an article? In other words, wouldn't it be a great load off my back if the copyright was in the publisher's name?*

A. No! A writer should never give up his copyright to another party when it is possible to keep it in his name. To give up copyright means you give up all legal rights to the work. Therefore, you could not benefit from any use of the article after the initial publication.

Book Contract

Q. *Does the royalty publisher's clause (on copyright) state that the publisher shall obtain the copyright but that copyright shall be in the name of the author and shall be that author's property? Where might I obtain an agreement contract from a royalty publisher for observation?*

A. Most royalty contacts do set up an agreement whereby the publisher takes out the copyright in the name of the author. The publisher merely handles the paperwork on behalf of the author and the copyright is the author's property. If you glance through a sampling of current bestsellers, you'll find that it is the author's name that usually follows the copyright symbol. Publishers don't make a practice of sending out sample contracts for study, but you could always verify this point on any contract offered to you before you sign it. A sample domestic book contract is available for 75c and a No. 10 self-addressed stamped envelope from the Society of Author's Representatives, 10 Astor Place, 3rd floor, New York, NY 10003. (New York State residents add 8¼% sales tax.)

Rights vs Copyright

Q. When I sell various rights to my work, doesn't that affect my ownership of the copyright?

A. No. Various rights are all part of your copyright, but selling them in no way diminishes your ownership of the actual work. William Strong, in *The Copyright Book*, likens copyright to ownership of land. "If you own a parcel of land, you can sell mineral rights to A, water rights to B, and a right-of-way to C, and still be considered the owner of the underlying property," he writes. In the case of written work, you may sell paperback reprint rights to one company, film and television rights to another, and book club rights to still another without impairing your ownership of the original work.

Edited Manuscript Still Mine?

Q. When an editor tightens up my article, correcting a weak ending and other flaws, is the resultant article still under my copyright?

A. Yes. Usually an editor's changes in your manuscript will not be extensive enough to qualify as a new work derived from your own. However, if your work is going to be heavily revised, you should clarify with the editor that the article is still yours, not his.

Humor Collection

Q. For the last fifteen years I have been collecting jokes, riddles, funny sign slogans, and humorous writings. I've gathered these from friends, acquaintances, and therapists. I don't have a clue as to their origins, and I don't know if they are copyrighted or in the public domain. My problem is this: I am attempting to write a book (probably paperback length) incorporating the idea that a little humor in one's life will make the rough road of rehabilitation a little easier. Since I can't identify the author of some of these masterpieces of humor, how can I protect myself against possible plagiarism suits?

A. Short gags and jokes cannot be copyrighted, so you wouldn't have any difficulty in assembling those in a book. Two hundred- to three hundred-word short prose humor pieces, however, might present a problem. If they did appear originally in copyrighted publications, you would have to rewrite them substantially to avoid plagiarism.

Rights Infringement

Q. Since ideas can't be copyrighted, would it be necessary to obtain permission from the author of a short story before expanding the material to book length?

A. You are not at liberty to base a book on another author's short story without the consent of that author, since he has the exclusive right of adaptation of his own work. If you're only using the theme off or crime does not) and not the actual characters and other aspects of the story, then you're only using the idea and you can proceed without permission.

Copyright Titles?

Q. *Does the new copyright law give copyright protection to titles? Is it legal for me to use an article title that is already the title of a published book?*

A. It is not possible to copyright titles, so you can use the title of a book for an article title. If you used it for another *book*, however, you could be challenged with unfair competition.

Reusing Articles in a Book

Q. *The book on which I'm working relies heavily on information from articles I've written over the years. Only a handful of editors have given me permission; others have not replied. None of the checks I received in payment for the works indicated I signed away all rights. Can I use the material without infringing on the copyrights of the various publications involved?*

A. Since you never signed a check with a statement that you were selling all rights to your articles, and assuming the editors had not publicized in writer's magazines or *Writer's Market* a policy of buying all rights, you should be able to use material from them without being sued for copyright infringement.

Reuse Uncopyrighted Article?

Q. *In researching a magazine article, I came across an article in a magazine that I would like to use. The magazine was not copyrighted. Can I use this material?*

A. Since March 1, 1989 a copyright notice is not required to maintain the author's or a publication's copyright, so it is harder to tell whether the material is in the public domain or the publisher inadvertently left off the copyright notice. The safest thing to do would be to write the magazine and find out, requesting permission to use the material if it is copyrighted.

Canadian Copyright

Q. *If my work is published in Canada, will I need to register it there, too? How does Canadian copyright differ from U.S. copyright?*

A. Since Canada and the United States both belong to the Berne Copyright Convention, your Canadian-published work is protected just as if it were published in the U.S. Registration, as in the U.S., is optional, but advisable to prove ownership in the event of legal action. In general, U.S. and Canadian copyright laws are similar; the author having specific questions should contact the Copyright and Industrial Design Branch, 50 Victoria St., Place Portage, Tower One, Hull, Quebec K1A 0C9.

Copyright Duration

Q. *Once my work is copyrighted, for how long is it protected?*

A. For works copyrighted on or after January 1, 1978, copyright protection lasts for the rest of the author's life and for fifty years after his death. If the work is collaborative, the death of the last surviving collaborator determines the starting point for the fifty years. If the work was produced under a pen name or anonymously, or if it is a work made for hire, copyright expires seventy-five years after first publication, or one hundred years after its first creation, whichever is earlier.

"Publication" and Public Domain

Q. *What's the difference under the present copyright law as opposed to the old law regarding "published" and "unpublished" manuscripts and the public domain?*

A. Under the old law, if you distributed reproduced copies of your unpublished manuscript to the public—either through typed copies or mimeographed or other reproductions—you were considered to have "published" it. If you had not registered it for copyright and it did not contain a copyright notice, it fell into the public domain. Under the present law, your work is copyrighted as soon as you create it—whether you formally register it for copyright or not—but you must show your copyright notice on your original manuscript and any reproduced copies for best protection.

Publishing Old Letters

Q. *I found some fascinating letters from one of my relatives who fought in the Civil War, and I would like to incorporate some of these in a book I'm doing. Am I free to use these?*

A. Not without permission from his heirs. While the physical piece of paper that is a letter may be the property of the recipient, the thoughts and ideas expressed in it still belong to the creator—or his heirs, if he is deceased.

Public Broadcasting and the Use of Copyrighted Materials: What We Know So Far*

The procedures for implementing the Copyright Act of 1976 are now being established under provisions set forth in the law. What follows is a summary of the statutory language upon which these procedures will be based.

Effective Date of Law:
Powers of Copyright Royalty Tribunal: Upon nomination and confirmation. Other provisions: January 1, 1978.

This outline was prepared by David Gillmore, former General Manager, Instructional Television Services, Marshall University, Huntington, West Virginia.

"Fair Use" of Copyrighted Works:
Excerpts from copyrighted works can usually be used in public radio and television programs *without* prior clearance or royalty payment. Check full provisions in the law.
In instances where "fair use" does not apply, see below.

Audio-Visual Works: Visual presentations, together with accompanying audio, if any. Examples: motion pictures, television programs, filmstrips.
    1. Prior clearance required.
    2. Royalty payment may be required.

Literary Works:
Dramatic: (Includes dramatic presentations of nondramatic works.)
    1. Prior clearance required.
    2. Royalty payment may be required.
Non dramatic:
    1. Prior clearance required.
    2. Royalty payment may be required. Negotiations are continuing to simplify clearance procedure.

Music Performed on a Program: Nondramatic musical *compositions* performed on a program. (See also "Sound Recordings.")
No prior clearance required.

Pictorial Works: Photographs; graphics; sculpture.
    1. No prior clearance required.
    2. Blanket fee to cover public broadcasting currently under negotiation.

Sound Recordings: The audio *performance* of nondramatic works recorded on discs, tapes, etc.
    1. No prior clearance required.
    2. No royalty payment required.
Notes:
    1. Does *not* apply to audio from audiovisual works.
    2. If music, see *also* "Music" above.

Special Exemptions
from Clearance and Royalty Provisions:

Instructional Broadcasts: Nondramatic literary, pictorial, or musical works may be performed or displayed *without* prior clearance or royalty payment *if*:

1. The program is a regular part of systematic instructional activities of a governmental body or nonprofit educational institution.
2. The work is directly related and of material assistance to the teaching content of the program.
3. The primary audience is a group of regularly enrolled students.
4. No more than thirty copies of the program exist at any one time.
5. The program is erased after seven years.

Literary Material for the Handicapped:
The following uses are exempt from prior clearance and royalty payment:
Nondramatic Material—Radio (AM, FM, or SCA):
1. Program must be specifically designed for and primarily directed to the visually handicapped.
2. No more than ten copies of the program may exist at any one time.

Television:
1. Program must be specifically designed for and primarily directed to the hearing impaired.
2. No more than ten copies of the program may exist at any one time.

Dramatic Literary Material—Radio (SCA *only*):
1. Program must be specifically designed for and primarily directed to the visually handicapped.
2. The dramatic work must be at least ten years old.
3. The work may be given by same group of performers one time only.
4. The work may be broadcast by a given station one time only.
5. The work may be broadcast on SCA *only*.

Chapter 8
Protecting Your Ideas in Hollywood

Lionel S. Sobel

Deserved or not, the movie and television industries have a reputation for stealing ideas. This chapter will help you calculate the risks you take when submitting ideas to producers and how to protect those ideas. It tells:

1. Why a movie or television show based on an idea similar to yours probably is just a coincidence.

2. Why laws governing contracts and confidential relationships may offer more protection than copyright law.

3. Why blurting out an idea to a producer may mean you can't protect yourself if that idea is used without your permission.

4. How an agent can help.

"Hollywood." The word itself evokes thoughts of movies, television, and palm trees . . . as well as Oscars, Emmys, and money. In the last thirty years, has there lived a writer (published or aspiring) who has not thought, at least once, about doing some work for the studios? Not likely, and small wonder. Those who write for the purpose of communicating with others cannot ignore this fact: More people view a *poorly* watched network television program than see (let alone read) the front pages of the *Los Angeles Times* and *New York Times* combined.

Movie and television producers do business with lots of writers and pay many of them very well. Not all the writers are ensconced in bungalows on studio lots, however, nor would all of them want to be. Many do not even write scripts; they write books, articles, stories, "treatments," proposals, and idea sketches. In other words, they write the raw material from which movie and television producers begin to manufacture their products. Professional screenwriters—those whose names are seen when the credits roll—are merely the tip of the iceberg. Writers who reach the tip almost always are represented by agents and lawyers who look after the business and legal details of their craft. This chapter is for the others: those who are still working their way to the tip, and those who prefer to toil outside of Hollywood itself.

The process of making movies and television programs begins when a producer acquires the rights to a "property." In most places, "property" means land. But in Hollywood, it is short for "literary property" and means something out of which a movie or show can be developed. Acquiring rights to a property is a ritual involving negotiations and contracts and, in many cases, nervousness on both sides.

Protecting Your Ideas

The reason for this nervousness is that rights cannot be acquired unless and until a producer is shown a writer's property. Once disclosed, however, properties can be stolen more easily than apples from a supermarket. Indeed, the fact that a property has been stolen may not become apparent until the movie or television program is released, by which time all the writer is left with is an expensive lawsuit. That is why writers are frequently nervous. Hollywood has a reputation—not entirely deserved—as a place where properties are often stolen.

There is another side to the coin, however. It is simply a fact of life that the ideas that are most likely to be used in making movies and television programs are those that are similar to already successful films and shows. William Goldman explained, with apparent anguish and aggravation, exactly why this is so in his bestselling book *Adventures in the Screen Trade*. A similar explanation, in business and economic terms, appears in a multivolume legal treatise entitled *Entertainment Law* by New York City lawyers Thomas Selz and Melvin Simensky. In brief, the explanation is that not a single person in Hollywood can unfailingly predict which projects will be successful. Thus, in order to minimize financial risk, new projects tend to mirror others that have been successful. This is why many similar—but independently developed—ideas are often considered by producers.

Coincidences Do Occur

The frequency with which similar stories are independently created is surprising to those who have not worked in Hollywood (and to many who have). Remarkable coincidences have been documented, however. In 1979, a Los Angeles jury returned a $185,000 verdict in favor of sixty-eight-year-old manicurist Bernice Mann against Warren Beatty, screenwriter Robert Towne, and Columbia Pictures. The jury concluded that the movie *Shampoo* had been based on a twenty-nine-page outline Mann had written from her experiences as a beauty salon employee. The outline contained brief descriptions of a half-dozen principal characters in a beauty salon setting and a short narration for a number of scenes. Mann had given a copy of her outline to a friend, who gave it to a neighbor, who gave it to a friend who was a production manager for a company that was then based at Columbia. The production manager gave it to a story editor employed by his own company, and it was never returned.

Shampoo was released by Columbia several years later and contained a number of elements that also appeared in Mann's outline. Both included beauty salon settings, homosexual hairdressers, a hairdresser's sexual exploits, a mother-daughter competition involving sexual accusations, a shampoo girl, and a scene in which a hairdresser was interrupted while working on a woman involved in a political gathering that evening. Given these similarities, how many writers would not feel their material had been stolen?

When the jury's verdict was read, the press had a field day. Bernice Mann, the heroine, had defeated the "big shots" from Hollywood to win her just compensation and recognition. About a month later, however, another event occurred in the case—one that was given much smaller headlines. The judge who had presided over the trial set aside the jury's verdict and entered judgment for Beatty and his fellow defendants. The judge did so, he explained, because he found that Robert Towne's script had been independently created and was not in fact based on Mann's outline at all. What made the judge come to this conclusion?

Lots of things. The story editor who had been given Mann's outline did not work for Columbia; he worked for an independent production company that was merely using space on the Columbia lot. Furthermore, Columbia proved that it had never received a copy of Mann's outline. Neither Beatty nor Towne had ever met or talked with the story editor before Mann's lawsuit was filed. Finally, Towne proved that he first began working on the script for *Shampoo* six years before Mann's outline had been given to the story editor. And Towne actually submitted his script to Columbia a full year before Mann's outline was given to the story editor. Mann appealed the dismissal of her case, but it was affirmed by the appellate court.

As this case proves, coincidences do occur. Just as writers are concerned that their material will be stolen, producers are concerned that more than one writer will claim to be the author of the property on which that producer's project was based. History has shown that producers have reason to be concerned. For example, the makers of the movie *Coming Home*—including Jane Fonda—were sued by two different and unrelated novelists, both of whom contended that the movie was based on their book. Fonda and her fellow defendants won both of those cases, but not without spending time and energy on each.

Protection Under Copyright Law

Fortunately for writers and producers alike, the law provides each with a measure of protection. The law's protection allows writers to offer their material for sale, confident that their material cannot be stolen with impunity. The law's protection also allows producers to look at properties, confident that they will not be liable to every writer whose work they consider. Exactly which legal principle applies in a particular case depends on the *nature* of the writer's work and the *manner* in which it was submitted to the producer.

Consider first the *nature* of the writer's work. Books of course have long been a fertile source for movies and television programs. Book publishers frequently have subsidiary rights departments staffed by executives whose specific job it is to sell movie and television rights to producers. In recent years, magazine articles and even songs have been made into movies and television programs. All of these kinds of works—books, articles, and songs—are protected by the federal Copyright Act. As a result of this protection, the copyright owner (which is the author, unless the author has sold the copyright to someone else) has the exclusive right to copy the work and to make derivative works from it. A derivative work is one based on a preexisting work, and motion pictures are specifically mentioned by the Copyright Act as an example of derivative works.

Since January 1, 1978, when the current Copyright Act took effect, even unpublished literary works have been protected by the federal Copyright Act, as much so as published books and articles. In fact, literary works are protected by copyright from the moment they are written down, even if the author does not register his or her claim to copyright with the Copyright Office in Washington, D.C. In other words, although copyrights *may* be registered in Washington before works are published, prepublication registration is *not* required for copyright protection. Indeed, it is not actually necessary to register a copyright unless and until it becomes necessary to file suit against an infringer, though there are certain advantages (concerning the amounts of money that may be recovered in an infringement lawsuit) to registering one's copyright before it is infringed.

Some Material Isn't Protected

Clearly, the Copyright Act is an important aspect of entertainment law that protects writers in their dealings with producers. Copyright protects not only published authors, but also those who have written unpublished scripts, stories, and treatments. Copyright does not protect everything that is written, however. It does not protect, for example, ideas or concepts. Nor does it protect theories or facts. Copyright only protects a writer's particular "expression"—meaning the writer's plot, characters (if they are sufficiently developed and unique), and exact words. Furthermore, copyright protection only prohibits the unauthorized making of a "substantially similar" work. Similarities which are less than "substantial" do not run afoul of the Copyright Act. Some examples may help to illustrate these principles.

One of the leading cases in this area of entertainment law was filed by A. A. Hoehling, the author of the book *Who Destroyed the Hindenburg?*, against Universal City Studios, the company that produced the movie *The Hindenburg*. In his lawsuit, Hoehling alleged that Universal had copied the plot of his account of the 1937 disaster that destroyed the German dirigible. Hoehling also charged that Universal had copied his research, as well as facts, certain phrases, and scenes from his book. Hoehling's book had propounded the theory that a Hindenburg crew member had sabotaged the lighter-than-air craft—a theory that Universal's movie relied on as well. But the court held that even if Universal had copied Hoehling's theory and certain other elements of his book, copyright infringement had not been proved. This was because theories and historical facts are not protected by copyright, the court explained. Moreover, the scenes which Hoehling accused Universal of copying—such as those in a German beer hall—were held to be stock or standard literary devices, and as such, not protectible either.

The producers of the popular television series *WKRP in Cincinnati* were the defendants in another interesting and instructive case. The plaintiffs in this case were writers Salvatore Giangrasso and Steve Peitrofesa who in 1976 wrote and copyrighted a four-page script for a situation comedy series. The proposed series featured the staff of a fictional radio station, including its disc jockeys, news staff, engineer, and owner. The script for the pilot episode involved a remote broadcast from the business premises of an advertiser that is interrupted by an armed robber.

WKRP in Cincinnati was first broadcast by CBS in 1978. WKRP also was a fictional radio station, and the program also featured a staff of disc jockeys, a newsman, an owner, and on at least one occasion, an engineer. Furthermore, one episode involved a remote broadcast from the business premises of an advertiser that is interrupted by an armed man. In their suit, Giangrasso and Peitrofesa alleged that this episode infringed the copyright to their script.

The court, however, disagreed. It explained that "the essence of infringement lies in a taking not of a general theme but in its particular expression through similarities of treatment, details, scenes, events, and characterizations." Applying this legal principle, the court ruled that even if the producers of *WKRP* had "copied the idea of a remote broadcast interrupted by a robber with a gun, such copying is not actionable because it is only of an idea, and the handling, scenes, details, and characterizations used by plaintiffs and defendants in their works based on this idea are unquestionably not substantially similar."

In its decision dismissing the case, the court detailed why the two works were not substantially similar. The court noted that in the plaintiffs' script, the armed robber wanted money, whereas in the

WKRP episode the armed man was an out-of-work radio announcer who merely wanted to get on the air to demonstrate his ability. In the plaintiffs' script, the radio announcer is so oblivious to what is going on that he does not even realize that the robber is armed or is committing a robbery. In *WKRP*, the disc jockey is not only aware of what is going on, he sympathizes with the armed man and helps him escape capture by the police. Other similarities were found to be nothing more than "*scenes a faire*," that is, scenes which would necessarily appear in programs about a certain idea. Among these were scenes in which the radio station's advertisers do pitches on the air, scenes in which guns are used and the police arrive, and countdowns before the remote broadcast begins. The plaintiffs admitted that there was no literal similarity of expression in these scenes, and thus they did not establish an infringement either.

Finally, the plaintiffs claimed that the characters in *WKRP* were similar to the characters in their script. On this issue, the court said, the plaintiffs would have to suffer the penalty authors must bear when they fail to develop their characters fully. "The less developed the characters, the less they can be copyrighted," the court explained. In this case, the plaintiffs' characters were mere types with little development beyond their positions at the station. Moreover, the characters in *WKRP* who held comparable positions were found to have different traits than those described by the plaintiffs in their script.

These principles of law also were applied in the two *Coming Home* cases mentioned earlier. Both the novels written by the plaintiffs in those two cases dealt with war and its effects on soldiers and their loved ones, just as did the movie. In both cases, however, the courts held that these similarities, as well as certain others, were mere ideas and *scenes a faire*, neither of which are protected by copyright.

Other Kinds of Protection

Although copyright does not protect a writer's ideas, other principles of entertainment law sometimes do. The circumstances have to be right, however. If they are, even uncopyrightable ideas may be protected by contract or confidential relationship. The legal theory involved is this: If a writer *discloses* a movie or television idea to a producer in exchange for the producer's *promise* to pay for the idea if the producer *uses* it, the writer and producer have entered into a *contract*. As a result, if the producer does use the writer's idea, the producer is legally obligated to pay for it. Similarly, if a writer discloses a movie or television idea to a producer *in confidence*, in reliance on the producer's *promise* not to use *or disclose* the idea to anyone else unless the idea is paid for, then the producer is legally obligated to pay for the idea if he uses it or discloses it to anyone else who does.

The producer's promise not to use or disclose the writer's idea without paying for it does *not* have to be in writing. Naturally, writers have an easier time proving that the producer made such a promise when the promise is in writing. But in some cases, courts have *implied* the existence of a promise to pay merely from the circumstances surrounding the writer's disclosure of his or her idea.

Uniqueness May Be an Issue

The law is unclear whether the writer's idea must be unique and novel in order to qualify for protection under contract and confidential relationship principles, or whether commonplace ideas qualify as well. This very question was at the heart of a recent case involving one of the most successful television series of all time, *The Cosby Show*. After the show premiered on NBC in the fall of 1984, an NBC employee named Hwesu Murray reminded the network that in 1980—four years before the series went on the air—he had submitted a written proposal for a half-hour situation comedy to be entitled "Father's Day" that—like *The Cosby Show*—was to "focus upon the family life of a Black American family." "The leading character" in Murray's proposed show was to have been "the father . . . a devoted family man and a compassionate, proud, authority figure." Moreover, Murray had specifically recommended that Bill Cosby be hired to play the father.

Television viewers now know that Murray's suggestion was a good one. But in 1980, NBC apparently thought otherwise. The network returned his proposal with a letter saying, "We are not interested in pursuing [its] development at this time." Naturally, when NBC did begin broadcasting *The Cosby Show* in 1984, Murray concluded its "time" had come. And he was very disappointed that he had not been offered credit or compensation for its creation. He was, in fact, disappointed enough to sue.

Murray filed his lawsuit in New York where NBC has its headquarters and where *The Cosby Show* is produced. Thus, New York law controlled the outcome of the case. According to the courts that heard Murray's case, this meant that his ideas had to be *novel* in order to be protected. While Murray's ideas were good—the success of *The Cosby Show* itself proves that—they were not "novel," the courts held, for many reasons. As Murray himself had acknowledged in his original proposal, the show he suggested resembled shows already on the air, such as *Father Knows Best* and *The Dick Van Dyke Show*. Although those programs had portrayed white families, while Murray's was to portray a black family, the networks had cast black actors, including Bill Cosby himself, in earlier series. Moreover, the idea of combining a family situation comedy theme with a black cast had been publicly suggested by Bill Cosby, in a newspaper interview published back in 1965—fifteen years before Murray had proposed that same idea. Since Murray's ideas were not novel, the law of New York did not protect them, under contract or confidential relationship principles, or any others.

On the other hand, the law of California does not appear to require "novelty" in order to protect ideas. For example, in one well-known entertainment case, a California appellate court held that the idea to cast Elizabeth Taylor and Richard Burton in a movie version of Shakespeare's *The Taming of the Shrew* was a protectible idea, even though movie versions of it had been made before with husband-and-wife stars in the leading roles, and even though Burton himself had previously appeared in a movie version of another Shakespeare work, *Hamlet.*

However, even those judges who have not required novelty limit idea protection to those cases where the writer proves that he or she was the source from which the producer actually got the idea. If the idea is commonplace, this may be a very difficult thing to prove, because commonplace ideas float around Hollywood all the time and often come to producers from many different sources.

Producer Must Have Chance to Say No

Some things are clear about the protection of a writer's ideas. One of these is that the producer must be given an opportunity to reject the writer's offer to disclose an idea. In other words, the writer cannot blurt out an idea to an unsuspecting producer. If the writer does so, no judge will imply the existence of a contract or confidential relationship, and the producer will be able to use the writer's idea without paying anything for it. Upon reflection, this may seem obvious. Door-to-door salespeople, for example, cannot leave unordered merchandise on homeowners' doorsteps and then insist that those homeowners either pay for the merchandise or return it. By law, any salesperson foolish enough to have done so simply has made a gift of that merchandise, which the homeowner may pay for, or not, as he or she wishes. The same is true of the foolish writer who blurts out an idea before the producer has an opportunity to decline to hear it. This principle of entertainment law has a practical effect on how writers should submit unsolicited ideas to producers—an effect that will be discussed below.

Another point that is clear about the law of idea protection is this: Contract and confidential relationship principles protect writers only against unauthorized use of their ideas by producers they have dealt with directly. *Copyright* protection—in cases where it is available— does prohibit the unauthorized use of a writer's material by anyone, including complete strangers who may read the writer's work, without the writer even knowing about it, thousands of miles away from where the writer lives and works. But contract and confidential relationship principles do not protect writers against the unauthorized use of their ideas by producers who got those ideas from someone other than the writers themselves.

This principle was important in the *Shampoo* case, because Beatrice Mann gave her outline to a friend, who gave it to a neighbor, who gave it to a friend, who gave it to a story editor, who gave it—Mann thought—to Columbia or Warren Beatty or Robert Towne. Even if the story editor had given the outline to Columbia or Beatty or Towne (something which they proved did not occur), Mann would not have been able to establish either a contract or a confidential relationship with any of them. This principle too has a practical effect on how writers should submit their ideas to producers.

An Agent May Be the Answer

What then should writers do to protect their material? Unfortunately, the best advice is also the worst advice, for most new writers. Get a reputable agent and let the agent deal with producers. This is the best advice for several reasons. Agents make it their business to know what kinds of projects particular producers are most interested in developing. Thus an agent has the ability to match a writer's material with producers who are most likely to be interested in it. Producers themselves prefer to deal with agents rather than writers, because agents prescreen material and submit only professional quality work. Furthermore, producers get fewer infringement and theft-of-ideas claims from writers who are represented by agents—though there are those who say that this is because producers are less likely to steal material from a writer who is represented by an agent than from one who is not.

The reason that "get an agent" is the worst advice for most new writers—or at least not very helpful advice—is they usually find it more difficult to get an agent than to get a producer to consider their material. How does the writer get an agent? A list of those who will work with previously unproduced writers appears in *Writer's Market*. The writer can also obtain a list from the Writers Guild of America, 8955 Beverly Boulevard, Los Angeles, CA 90048, although it doesn't say whether the agent deals only with established writers.

Writers who do not have agents should not be afraid to submit their material to producers directly, despite fears of infringement and idea theft. "Nothing ventured, nothing gained" is after all an accurate platitude. Furthermore, there are specific steps writers can take to obtain legal protection for their material—steps which should give them enough peace of mind to deal with producers on their own, at least until success brings them an agent's added clout.

Establish Date of Creation

Published material differs from unpublished material in one potentially important respect. It is easier for a writer to prove—if need be—that his or her published work was crated *before* a producer's movie or television program. This is because it is usually easy to prove the date of publication.

It can be more difficult to prove the date on which unpublished material was created. This very difficulty resulted in the dismissal of a suit against Lucasfilm, Ltd., the producer of the 1980 movie *The Empire Strikes Back.* In this case, a graphic artist named Lee Seiler claimed that in 1976 he had created designs for the giant machines that later appeared as the Imperial Walkers in *Empire.* Unfortunately for Seiler, his original drawings were "lost or destroyed," and thus, after the movie was released in 1980, he "reconstructed" his drawings and sought to use the reconstructions to prove what his 1976 drawings looked like. However, the courts refused to allow him to do so. "The dangers of fraud in this situation are clear," the judge explained. Without his original drawings, Seiler had no evidence; and without evidence, he had no case.

The lesson taught by *The Empire Strikes Back* case is clear. Writers who wish to submit unpublished material to producers should first take steps to create evidence of the date by which their material was created. Writers can do this in one of two ways.

One is to make use of the Writers Guild of America Registration Service. Registration of a work with the Writers Guild does not create any legal rights. It does, however, enable writers to prove the date by which they created registered material. This is because registered material is kept on file by the Writers Guild for ten years, and if the writer wishes to renew the registration, for an additional ten years. In the event there is a dispute concerning the date by which a registered work was created, a representative of the Writers Guild is available to testify to the date on which the registered copy was deposited. The fee is $15 per deposit for nonmembers. Information and instructions for using the registration service are available from the Writers Guild of America at 8955 Beverly Boulevard, Los Angeles, CA 90048, or at 555 West 57th Street, New York, NY 10019.

The other preferred method by which writers can establish evidence of the date by which their material was created is to register the copyright with the Copyright Office. Registration of an unpublished work requires the deposit of a copy of the work. Thus the deposited copy and the date of its registration are available to prove the date by which the work was created. The fee is $10 per registration. Forms and instructions are available from the Register of Copyrights, Library of Congress, Washington DC 20559.

In order to take advantage of contract and confidential relationship principles to protect ideas and avoid "blurting out" those ideas, it is necessary for the producer to have an opportunity to decline the writer's disclosure. So writers who submit material by mail usually are asked to sign a statement that reads something like this example.

Dear Writer,

Every year, we consider literally hundreds of ideas, proposals, manuscripts, articles, and books for the purpose of determining whether they may be suitable for development into motion pictures or television programs. Frequently, we receive similar materials from more than one source. Because of lawsuits against members of our industry that have been filed by those who believe that their material has been used without authorization, we have become extremely reluctant to consider unsolicited submissions such as yours. Therefore, if you wish us to consider your material, we must ask you to sign the enclosed copy of this form. By doing so, you agree that in exchange for our reading of your submission, you waive and release us from any legal or equitable claims you otherwise might have against us on account of our use, or alleged use, of your material. Should we wish to use your material, we will be happy to discuss with you a mutually agreeable price for it. But please be aware that by signing this form, you are agreeing that we shall have the right to use your material even if you and we cannot agree on a price for it, and you shall not have the right to prevent us from doing so or the right to recover anything from us should we do so.

Very truly yours,

Producer

(Signed)

When writers receive letters of this sort, they must decide whether to gamble on the producer's honesty and good faith. One way to do this is to deal only with reputable, well-established producers whose integrity can be trusted.

Review/Chapter 8

Copyright law is designed to protect a writer's plot, characters, and exact words—that writer's particular "expression" of an idea. It does not protect:
   ✔ideas or concepts
   ✔theories
   ✔facts
   ✔*scenes a faire*, or scenes that would necessarily appear in scripts about a certain plot
   Contract and confidential relationships law may protect some ideas that aren't covered by copyright. However, there are some limitations:

✔the producer must be given the chance to decline to hear the idea

✔usually only people you've dealt with directly are bound by these laws

✔in some states, the idea must be unique and novel in order to qualify

Writers can decrease the chances that their work will be used without authorization by:

✔using an agent to submit ideas to producers

✔establishing the date of creation by registering the work with the Writers Guild

✔registering the copyright with the Copyright Office

Chapter 9
Your First Book Contract

Georges Borchardt

The first time a publisher offers you a book contract, you may be overwhelmed by all the decisions you're being asked to make—decisions that can affect not only that book but other projects in the future. How do you know what's standard publishing practice, what's fair as an advance, what clauses may limit your rights to your own work? This chapter will tell you:

1. What average advances are and how they're paid.

2. How royalties are calculated, and why some fine print can affect your royalty earnings.

3. What rights other than publishing the hardcover version are being negotiated and how these rights are usually handled.

4. What the publisher's responsibilities are, including time restraints for publishing the book and requirements for when and how you're paid.

At no time are you, as a writer, more vulnerable than when you're confronted with your first book contract. At last you're being "recognized." For months, perhaps years, you may have been the only one with faith in your own work; you may, in fact, have been willing to pay a publisher to get published. Now, all of a sudden, someone else has faith in you and is willing to pay you. Where will you summon the nerve to ask any questions, to bargain with your benefactor? You will need strength, or a literary agent, or both. And the following hints might be of help to you.

Most publishers have their own printed contract forms, on which little is left to be filled out besides the agreed-upon advance and royalty rates. It is this form you will be sent by your publisher, with a request that you sign on the last page. Many writers sign the form without reading it, or without understanding it, and they often come to regret it. They should go over each clause of the contract, try to understand what it means, then determine what is not in the contract that perhaps should be and what is in the contract that should not be. Some of the more important points are:

The Advance

The advance is the amount of money the publisher guarantees it will pay the author. It is sometimes paid in installments, but in the case of a completed manuscript it should be paid in full on signing the contract. The size of the advance is an indication of the faith a publisher has in a book, and of the nature of its commitment. In some instances the advance is applied to royalties only, more often it is applied to all earnings by the author under the contract (including the author's share of subsidiary rights—see "other rights" below).

The advance should be nonreturnable, except in the case of a commissioned work that the author fails to deliver. But most contracts stipulate that the manuscript must be "satisfactory" to the publisher, leaving the latter free to publish or not publish, as well as free to reclaim the advance. If such a stipulation is left in the contract, it should at least be amended to read that you will reimburse the publisher only if you sell your book elsewhere, and only out of the proceeds of your new contract. Otherwise you might find yourself in the awkward position of being asked to refund money you spent long ago, and which you now cannot pay back.

Average Advances

What kind of advances can you expect?

On a juvenile book, it might be as little as $2,000; but on an adult trade book the advance may be $5,000 to $20,000 and often more. Rock-bottom advances on a novel or nonfiction book, hardcover or paperback still are $2,000 to $4,000. On commissioned books, the publisher usually pays half the advance on signing the contract, and half on delivery. Since authors need money while writing rather than when they are through, advances often are paid in more installments—say, one third on signing, one third on delivery of half the manuscript, and the balance on full delivery.

Royalties

Standard royalties on an adult trade book (as opposed to children's books or textbooks) are 10 percent of the retail price up to 5,000 copies sold, 12½ percent from 5,000 copies to 7,500 or 10,000 copies, and 15 percent thereafter.

Royalties on children's books are usually somewhat lower, depending on what kind of illustrations are involved, whether they are supplied by the author, etc. For example, where color illustrations are as important as the text, the royalty (10 to 12½ percent) would be divided 50/50 between the author and artist. For text with line drawings, 8 to 10 percent for the author and 2 percent for the artist would not be unusual. Where illustrations are minimal the publisher may simply pay a flat fee to the artist and the royalty to the author.

Royalties on textbooks at the college level could range from 8 percent to 19 percent of publisher's net receipts and at the elementary and secondary school level, 3 to 5 percent of net receipts.

Royalties Should Not Be "Net"

It is important to make sure that royalties are based on the retail price, rather than "net receipts." There is nothing essentially wrong with basing royalties on "net receipts" (the amount actually received by the publisher from bookstores or jobbers, rather than the amount charged customers by the bookstore) provided the royalty rates are increased sufficiently to make up for the discount granted by the publisher. In other words, a 15 percent royalty based on net receipts would correspond to a 9 percent royalty based on retail price, if we assume the average discount to the bookseller to be 40 percent.

It is also important to watch the fine print that follows the listing of the agreed-upon rates. All publishers pay lower rates on copies sold by mail order, or copies that are exported; but some also pay lower rates on copies sold at high discounts and their definitions of a high discount can vary by several percentage points. Under these special clauses, some publishers sell many more copies at exceptional (lower) rates than they do at the "regular royalty" rates originally negotiated with the author. Contracts of this type are misleading to the extent that they imply you will be paid higher royalties than you can actually expect to receive.

Finally, most publishers now have two retail prices for books, one including shipment costs to the bookstore (the price paid by the consumer) and one used as the basis for their invoice. It is usually on the latter price that the royalty is calculated under what publishers refer to as the freight pass-through clause. You should insist that the differential between the two "retail" prices not exceed 5 percent.

The "Other" Rights

In addition to publishing a hardcover edition (and the royalties listed above apply to such editions only), the publisher usually also has the right to publish a paperback edition. There are two kinds of paperback editions: the trade or quality paperbacks, which are sold in bookstores only, and the mass market paperbacks, which are sold in bookstores and also through a number of other outlets (drugstores, airports, etc.) Trade paperbacks are more expensive, are printed on better paper, and tend to have the same type as hardcover editions. Mass market paperbacks have inexpensive paper, contain more words on the page, and sell for less.

If the publisher publishes its own paperback edition, this will usually be trade paperback, on which the author will normally be paid a 7½ percent royalty (some contracts may call for only 5 or 6 percent) based on the retail price.

The publisher will also have the right to sublicense paperback rights to another publisher, usually (but not always) for a mass market edition, and will normally share the proceeds 50/50 with the author. We'll deal with this in more detail later.

You should ask for the right of approval of such sublicenses, as most publishers' contracts do not even obligate the publisher to inform you of a sublicense (or provide for your getting copies of your book in its new incarnation).

Sales to Book Clubs

The publisher will have the right to license book-club rights. The traditional division of proceeds is 50/50, where the book club pays an advance and royalties. Some smaller book clubs simply buy copies from the publisher to distribute to their members, and this may call for a different arrangement—possibly 10 to 15 percent of publisher's net receipts to the author.

Other Sub Rights

You can retain many of the other subsidiary rights, and you will if you're represented by an agent. These include the right to publish the book in England and the British Commonwealth, the right to publish the book in translation, motion picture and television rights, first serial rights (the right to publish in newspapers and magazines before book publication), and recording rights. However, without an agent you may not know what to do with these rights if you retain them, and the publisher may not let you retain them in the first place. In that event the publisher is entitled to a commission on the sale of each of these rights:

On British rights, where the usual agency commission is 15 percent, the publisher tends to ask for 20 percent.

On translation rights, where the usual agency commission is 20 percent, the publisher may ask for 25 percent.

On motion picture and TV rights or recording rights, as well as first serial rights, where the usual agency commission is 10 percent, the publisher will probably also ask for 10 percent.

Warning: While some agents charge commissions higher than the ones listed above, some publishers have been known to ask for as much as a 50 percent commission on the sale of these subsidiary rights. In addition, agents who work through subagents (in foreign countries, or in Hollywood) share their commission with the subagent, thereby not charging the author an extra fee, but publishers often hire subagents without absorbing the subagent's commission, thereby further reducing the author's share.

Additional warning: Your contract should clearly state that all rights not specifically mentioned, including rights not yet in existence, are reserved by, and are the property of, the author.

Mass Market Reprint Rights

A major source of revenue under most contracts will be from the sale of mass market editions. Advances paid by reprint houses now range from $2,000 to several million, and while the former is far more common than the latter, hardly a month goes by without some million-dollar deal. It may be unrealistic to think in such terms when signing your first contract, but some knowledge of what is involved might come in handy.

The traditional division of paperback earnings is 50/50, and applies to both the advance and the royalties earned by the paperback edition. At this point the division tends to be a matter up for negotiation, with a 60/40 split in the author's favor (on earnings in excess of $50,000 or $100,000) being not uncommon. The difference in the income to the author can be very large: If reprint rights in your book are sold for $200,000 your share "normally" would be $100,000, but on the basis of a 60/40 split it would be $120,000, and on the basis of a 67/33 split, $133,334. The standard mass market paperback royalty is 8 percent of the retail price on the first 100,000 or 150,000 copies sold and 10 percent thereafter. On a bestselling title, paperback royalties go as high as 15 percent.

Rights the Publisher Acquires

Some publishers buy an author's work outright, against a simple cash payment that represents all the author will earn from the book. For transactions of this sort, which I never recommend, most of what precedes and most of what follows does not apply. In general, however, publishers do not "buy" a book; they are simply acquiring certain rights, which are leased to them for a specific amount of time. In other words rights are "licensed" not "sold" to them.

The main right a publisher acquires is the right to publish the book, usually in hardcover, sometimes in paperback form—this should be clearly stated. The contract will also say where the publisher may sell the book, when its license expires, and what rights it acquires besides the right to publish the book.

The contract that will be sent to the author by the publisher will in all probability cover the right to publish in all languages, and throughout the world. If you wish to retain languages other than English, and the right to license your book separately in England (as you would if you were represented by an agent), then you should limit the grant to the English language, with exclusive publication rights limited to the United States and its possessions, Canada, and the Philippines. You can, of course, bargain with the publisher, granting additional rights in exchange for a higher advance.

The contract probably will also state that the rights licensed to the publisher are granted for the duration of the copyright. It is important for you to make sure that the contract states that should your

book go out of print at any time, and should the publisher not reprint it within a specified amount of time after having received a notice from you requesting him to do so, all rights granted will revert
to you.

Warning: The publisher's contract may state that the copyright will
be registered in the publisher's name, or in the publisher's and the
author's name. Make sure that this is amended to provide that the
copyright will be registered in the author's name, a request that will
practically always be granted, and that protects ownership of any reserved rights.

The Warranty Clause

The contract will ask you to guarantee certain things to the publisher, some of which should present no problems—that you are the
author of your book, that you haven't already licensed it to someone
else, and that you have not plagiarized—while other warranties
(dealing with libel and invasion of privacy) could drive you into bank-
ruptcy. Most warranty clauses are very sweeping: They make the author responsible for any costs incurred in defending suits, including
nuisance suits, and these costs can be enormous. The author should
only be liable where there has in fact been a judgment for damages,
and if possible the author's liability should be limited to a specific
amount. Most publishers now include authors in their liability insurance, but the cost of such insurance keeps rising, and so do the "de-
ductibles"; as a result you may get much less protection from this
insurance than you think. Ask the publisher to spell things out to
you as clearly as possible.

The Option Clause

Your publisher will ask for the right to have a chance at your next
book, which in most cases may seem fair. This is not so in all circumstances, however. If a publisher does a terrible job publishing
your first book, why should you have to subject your second book to
the same fate? Some option clauses state that the publisher may acquire your next book on the same terms as your first; some state
that the publisher need not make up its mind until several months
after it has published your first book.

Both of these stipulations should be avoided. The option to contract for your next book should be on terms to be agreed upon within
a stated period of time, and if it is a work of nonfiction the option
should be exercised on the basis of a synopsis, within a month of
submission. If the publisher and author cannot agree within the
stated period of time, the option should expire with no strings attached. Most authors cannot afford to embark on months of research
without the knowledge that they will be paid for their work. Do not
accept any restrictions as to when you may sign your next contract

(such as after publication of the book covered by the contract in hand).

The Publisher's Obligations

The contract submitted to you will tend to be longer on your obligations than on the publisher's. Having produced your book and handed it over to the publisher, however, you are certainly entitled to something in exchange. The main thing is, of course, to see your book published. While this seems rather obvious, oddly enough many publisher's contracts do not state when the publisher will publish the book (they may simply state "within a reasonable time").

It is normal to request that the book be published within twelve months of delivery of the final manuscript (publishers now need about nine months from delivery to publication, so this leaves them an additional three months to work out the best schedule for the book). While the contract should state whether the book will be published in hardcover or in paperback form, everything else (price, design, jacket copy, etc.) is usually left to the publisher.

How and When You're Paid

The contract should also state clearly how and when the author gets paid. Most publishers send statements twice a year (but some report only once a year), and make payments three months after the end of an accounting period. In other words, they pay on March 31 for earnings during the period of July 1 to December 31, which means they hold the author's money for anywhere from three to nine months. Some wait even longer. It is advisable to state in the contract that any substantial sums (e.g., more than $500) due the author from the licensing of subsidiary rights will be paid to the author within two weeks of receipt by the publisher, if the original advance has been earned out.

There are a number of other things a contract will cover, such as correcting proofs, receiving free copies of the book, etc., and we cannot deal with all of them here. There are also some special situations, such as the sale of a book to a mass market publishing house for original paperback publication, where some of these matters will work out differently.

Finally, an author should not expect the contract to solve all the problems that might arise. If you deal with an editor you trust and the editor remains with the publishing firm from when you sign the contract through the life of the book (admittedly a rare occurrence), you may not have to refer to your contract very often. The choice of a good editor and a good publishing house is at least as important as the contract. But even when you have made what you think is a perfect choice, at some point you may find that your contract, if it is a good one, is your only real friend.

Resources for Writers

Writers who have published one book within the previous seven years or three articles or stories in national magazines within the previous eighteen months may find it helpful to join the Authors Guild, 234 West 44th Street, New York, NY 10036. The guild has helpful information for members on book contracts and other author concerns. Dues are $75 per year.

There are two associations of literary agents: The Society of Authors' Representatives, 10 Astor Place, 3rd floor, New York, NY 10003 and the Independent Literary Agents Association, c/o Ellen Levine Literary Agency, 432 Park Ave. S., Suite 1205, New York, NY 10016. (A membership list is available from either for a self-addressed, stamped business-size envelope.)

A list of author's agents with details on types of material they handle appears in *Writer's Market*, published by Writer's Digest Books.

Sample book contracts are available from the Society of Authors' Representatives, same address as above, for 75 cents in stamps (U.S. publisher) and 50 cents in stamps (foreign publisher contract), plus a self-addressed, stamped envelope.

Review/Chapter 9

Advances indicate how much faith the publisher has in a book. When negotiating an advance, an author should try to make sure it is:

  ✔nonreturnable

  ✔paid in installments rather than the full amount on delivery

Royalties, the percentage of profit that is paid to the author, should be based on:

  ✔the book's retail price, not net receipts

  ✔an agreed-upon price, not discount prices the publisher offers special customers

  ✔a price that is no more than 5 percent less than the price paid by the customer

Among the other rights to be negotiated in a book contract are the rights to:

  ✔publish a paperback version of the book

  ✔sell the book to book clubs

  ✔sell the movie or television rights to the book

  ✔publish foreign-language versions

  ✔sell magazines the right to use excerpts

Other points to look for in your first book contract:

  ✔rights leased to the publisher should revert to the author if the book goes out of print

  ✔the copyright will be registered in the author's name

✔liability in the case of libel and invasion of privacy suits should be limited to successful suits

✔option clauses should not allow the publisher to acquire your next book under the same terms or to hold that book for an unlimited time

✔any substantial sum of money earned from the licensing of subsidiary rights will be paid within two weeks

Chapter 10
Trends in Subsidiary Rights

Perry H. Knowlton

Subsidiary rights—all those rights that go along with publishing a book, such as printing paperbacks and selling movie rights—can be an important source of income for writers. But the market for sub rights is always changing, and you need to keep on top of it if you want to make the most of sub rights sales. Here you'll catch up on the trends:

1. How the disappearance of some major magazine markets affects serial rights sales.

2. The outlook for paperback reprint sales.

3. How trends such as the growth in television movies and miniseries and the development of independent producers affect movie and TV sales.

4. What you can expect to earn from book-club sales.

5. Changes in the foreign markets for English books.

In book publishing today, the sale of subsidiary rights sometimes means the difference between profit or loss for the publisher, and fortune or anonymity for the writer.

The book contract sent the writer after the initial sale stipulates the terms governing publication and sale of the work, and it also defines many of the important areas of subsidiary rights. The territory granted to the publisher determines whether it will be handling foreign rights, and if the publisher is to do so, there will also be a clause governing the division of earnings from those rights. The same thing holds for other subsidiary rights—dramatic, radio, television, motion picture, and serial rights.

If the author is represented by an agent, most of these rights are in the agent's hands, and it's his or her responsibility to see that their potential is exploited in the author's best interests. This doesn't necessarily mean that subsidiary rights are sold to the highest bidder, for the selection of the best British or Italian publisher for any one particular book is more important than a possible difference in advances offered. The same factor enters into the sale of first serial rights, although to a lesser degree.

The agent almost invariably retains first serial rights, all foreign rights, and all performing rights (motion picture, television, radio, and stage) for the author. The publisher is traditionally granted, with occasional exceptions, the right to handle the licenses to paperback (also called softcover) reprints, book clubs, magazines and newspapers, anthologies, and other users after the initial publication of the book. The publisher has, in the past, traditionally expected and received 50 percent of earnings from these rights. Naturally, publishers claim that they must have this in order to make their usual profit. They would probably like to have a great deal more than 50 percent. Because of the split having been made from a traditional rather than a logical point of view, they have grown used to the income and find, like so many people who live up to their incomes, that they cannot afford to give it up without a fight. For the past twenty years or so, however, agents and authors have been able to arrange more favorable splits, given the proper leverage, of earnings from reprint licenses and, less often, from book-club licenses.

Paperback Reprints

All publishers will agree to some form of improvements over the flat 50 percent split on reprints which will be directly proportioned to the degree of their interest in the book or author in question. Some houses with wholly owned reprint subsidiaries like Simon and Schuster (Pocket Books), Putnam (Berkley), and in reverse, reprinters with hardcover facilities like Dell (now owned by Bantam), can arrange for the purchase of both hard and softcover rights in the original contract, paying over to the author full 100 percent royalties on the reprint edition. In making this kind of arrangement, the author loses the possibility of competitive bidding which could result in a larger advance guarantee, his or her share of which could be larger than the royalty eventually accumulating at the 100 percent rate.

Some bestselling authors with the necessary leverage have been able to separate completely their hardcover rights from their paperback rights. The hardcover publishers, in these instances, are willing to settle for hardcover publication rights. The authors then negotiate the terms of the reprint contracts on their own, getting healthy advances and royalties from each source with no splitting whatsoever.

Over the past few years a great many books have been originated by reprinters. The practice is not new. It started back about 1960, but recently it has become quite common. The reprinter commissions a work and then seeks a hardcover publisher, sometimes through the author's agent, sometimes on its own. The author usually retains 80 percent of hardcover earnings, though the reprinter will try to keep more than 20 percent.

Reprinters More Cautious

One serious problem for authors is that fewer paperback sales are being made. The average author of a first novel suffers today because reprinters are being more cautious in their acquisitions. Ten years ago a talented author of a first or second novel could pretty well count on a reprint sale, and equally important, so could his or her hardcover publisher. Hardcover publishers could usually count on the opportunity at least to cut their losses with a small reprint sale of $5,000. With diminishing opportunities to do so, the hardcover publisher is less likely to take a chance with a marginal book, so the author or his or her agent is finding it more difficult to place them.

Serial Sales Decreasing

In the area of first serial rights, the changes have been more dramatic and apparent. Forty years ago authors like Agatha Christie and Sinclair Lewis counted on making more money from first serial sales than from book publication. They depended on book publication for critical success, but the financial expectations from publication of the book were generally secondary to money earned from magazine use. Nowadays, quite obviously, the situation is completely reversed. The author of a book expects relatively little from first serial rights. The exception occurs, but the author no longer looks automatically to magazines as a major source of income.

Over the last three decades many major magazine markets disappeared—victims of mismanagement or changing concepts in the advertising business. The remaining magazines, facing decreasing competition in their own categories, are paying less and demanding more in return. They seem more and more to try to buy *all* serial rights rather than the traditional first North American rights, thereby depriving authors of potential income while at the same time paying less than previously. These days the value of magazine use of material from a book which is about to be published is more promotional than financial.

Movie Rights an Expanding Market

There is a great deal of money being spent and being made in the film industry. In 1987 the total number of films produced in the United States probably exceeded 500. Television is as important a market for the adaptation of novels as feature film. So-called long-form and miniseries—and more recently, HBO and other "made for cable" productions—have allowed for more generous budgets and much more lavish productions.

One of the factors in the growth of the film on TV has been the increasing acceptance of mature themes and subject matter. This is especially true for cable, since it is not subject to the restrictions imposed on regular broadcast television.

There are two points in the history of a novel (and the occasional work of nonfiction) that are usually best for pushing toward a sale. The decision as to which point to pick must be made as early as possible. Given a good film possibility, the agent must determine whether to sell it before publication and before much, if anything, is known about it in the industry, or to wait until after the book is out and established. A great many variables bear on the decision, but it comes down to whether the agent and/or author feel they can make a better sale before the book is out or after it is published.

Whether to allow studio story editors to get synopses in the studio files before officially offering the property is another factor to be considered. All major studios have story editors who, in order to earn their keep in their particular jobs, must provide synopses for every potential motion picture property which is published. The earlier and the quicker they provide coverage of these properties for the studios, the happier and safer they feel.

The quality of the synopsis rarely does justice to the book, and more often than not the tendency on the reader's part is to label the property with a negative tag since this is a great deal safer than a positive one. Later on when the true value of the book establishes itself, these synopses are in the files, and many an enthusiastic independent has run afoul of those early-bird synopses when he's gone to the studios for backing. Many an option has been dropped as a result. The galley-proof stage might already be too late to sell film rights, because the story editor's early-bird synopsis has often been hurriedly, and usually badly, written from a quick reading of galley proofs (or even manuscript copies) illicitly obtained from the printer, publisher, or some other source.

Studios, once the source of all good things and the prime movers in the industry, are no longer taking the lead in initiating film projects. The independent producers have virtually taken over the early development of properties, and one incidental effect has been to put increased pressure on agents to show material in the manuscript stage to potentially interested buyers.

Book Clubs

Selection of an author's book by a book club can mean extra income of a few hundred dollars (in the case of a specialized book and a small book club), to upwards of $200,000. Book-club royalties range from four and one-half cents per copy to 10 percent of the price at which the book club offers the book to its members. Guarantees may be based on expected sales of a few hundred copies to half a million copies. The Book-of-the-Month Club minimum guarantee is $50,000 to the publisher (which is then split with the author), and, of course, for big properties this price is negotiable. Their eventual earnings on each title almost invariably exceed the guarantee. Sometimes as much as twice the guarantee is earned.

At the Literary Guild, initial offers run between $50,000 and $75,000 for selections. Currently the Guild seems to be running only dual selections and occasionally triple selections. Alternate selections at both the BOMC and the Guild pay far less. The Junior Literary Guild guarantees on the average about $3,500; the Dollar Book Club guarantees on the average about $30,000. For the Reader's Digest Condensed Book Club, the earnings average from $50,000 to upwards of $100,000. Nonfiction usually earns less, and fiction more.

Commercial Rights

As toy makers, T-shirt manufacturers, and others search out popular book, movie, or TV characters to merchandise, the sale of "commercial rights" increases.

Often commercial rights are involved in adult books, both nonfiction and fiction, and agents are in a better position to determine what those rights are worth than the average author.

Foreign Rights

With a weak dollar, foreign publication rights are probably now more important than they have ever been. English language rights in the British Commonwealth have long been a good source of income for American authors, and that market continues pretty much as before.

Top Foreign Markets

Translation rights on the continent and in Japan, however, have been commanding more interest and better contracts. Despite the high cost incurred by the foreign publisher for commissioning a translation (as much as $8,000 for a novel of average length), major improvements in advances are noticeable in Germany, the Nordic countries, and Japan. In order of importance with respect to number of titles acquired for translation and average size of advances, the foreign publishing scene stacks up as follows: Germany, Japan, France, Italy, Sweden, Spain, Finland, Holland, Norway, Denmark, Brazil, Israel, Eastern Europe, and Greece.

In recent years there has been a surprising increase in the number of foreign languages in which bona fide translation contracts may be concluded: Catalan and Basque in Spain, Korean (since Korea signed an international copyright convention in 1987), Indonesian, and Chinese. Until recently Asia has been notorious for pirating books; however, this is now changing and the People's Republic of China will no doubt sign a copyright convention within the next year or two. With the advent of the Gorbachev regime and *perestroika* in the U.S.S.R there has been at best a small increase in the number of American books acquired by Soviet publishers for Russian language editions. The acute lack of hard currency in the Soviet Union and in the Eastern Bloc countries will continue to inhibit acquisition of American titles for the foreseeable future.

Earnings for an author from foreign rights can vary tremendously, ranging from next to nothing to many hundreds of thousands of dollars.

The unagented author will probably grant the handling of foreign rights to his or her publisher. The publisher, in turn, will probably turn this responsibility over to its agent for foreign rights, although a few handle the problem on their own. A good literary representative will tend the foreign publication rights of his or her authors with great care these days. There is more involved than the increasing market and growing advances, and more than the author's justifiable pride in being published all over the world. The shrinking of the world by jet travel and mass satellite communications has made international publication far more important than it was a few short years ago. Publishers of a novelist in Europe, England, and the United States, for instance, find that by near simultaneous publication and by careful trading back and forth of information dealing with a given novel, each publisher gains strength from the others, and the novel earns added support by the mere fact of its international publication.

The agent is the person who must be responsible for arranging this kind of cooperative effort, and he or she must act as the communications pipeline through which all useful information (news of sales, promotion, reviews, etc.) must flow to subagents and publishers.

Review/Chapter 10

If an author is represented by an agent, the subsidiary rights are often divided this way:

✔the agent, acting for the author, handles first serial rights, all foreign rights, and all performing rights

✔the publisher handles paperback reprints, book clubs, and other sales to magazines, newspapers, and anthologies

The past few years have brought these trends in the paperback reprints field:

✔some authors have been able to negotiate a more favorable deal than the traditional 50/50 split with the publisher

✔reprinters now often originate a book, then seek a hardcover publisher—instead of the other way around

✔reprinters have grown more cautious in deciding what to publish

Movie sales is an increasing market because:

✔the demand for television movies and miniseries has grown

✔the growth of cable channels has also produced an increased demand for scripts

✔acceptance of mature themes in film and TV has increased

The weak dollar has made foreign publication rights more important. Trends in this area are:

✔English language rights in the British Commonwealth continue to be a good source of income

✔translation rights in Europe and Japan are attracting more attention

✔new markets, such as translations into Korean, Indonesian, and Chinese, are opening

Chapter 11
Other Writing Contracts

Authors who write in forms other than books also need to look out for themselves before signing any contract. Whether you're already writing in these fields or are just considering expanding, this chapter will help. It gives you:

1. Guidelines for royalties paid to playwrights under the Dramatists Guild contract in New York.

2. Rate schedules negotiated by the Writers Guild for motion picture and television writing.

Playwrights

The Approved Production Contract for Dramatic Works, as negotiated by the Dramatists Guild with the League of American Theaters and Producers, calls for a royalty to the playwright of 5 percent of the Gross Weekly Box Office Receipts, going to 10 percent after recoupment of production expenses. The Approved Production Contract for Musicals provides for a royalty of 4.5 percent of the Gross Weekly Box Office Receipts going to 6 percent after recoupment.

Membership in the Dramatists Guild (234 W. 44th St., New York, NY 10036) is available in two forms. Active members must have had a production of one of their plays (Broadway, Off-Broadway or mainstage regional); dues are $75 per year or a percentage of one's first class royalties. Associate members need only have written one full-length play; dues are $50 per year. Subscribers membership is open to those persons interested in the theater, who are not playwrights; dues are $50 per year.

TV and Film

In 1988, the WGA negotiated a new four-year contract with all the TV and motion picture production companies, including the three networks. The new rate schedules that were established for screenplays are shown.

WGA 1988 Theatrical and Television Basic Agreement
Theatrical Compensation

Employment, Flat Deals +

	First Period Effective 8/8/88–8/31/89	
	Low	High
A. Screenplay, Including Treatment	$26,900	$50,023
Installments:		
Delivery of Treatment	10,086	15,375
Delivery of First Draft Screenplay	12,104	23,063
Delivery of Final Draft Screenplay	4,709	11,585
B. Screenplay, Excluding Treatment	16,810	34,591
Installments:		
Delivery of First Draft Screenplay	12,104	23,063
Delivery of Final Draft Screenplay	4,706	11,528
C. Additional Compensation for Story Included in Screenplay	3,846	7,687
D. Story or Treatment	10,086	15,375
E. Original Treatment	13,928	23,063
F. First Draft Screenplay, With or Without Option For Final Draft Screenplay		
First Draft Screenplay	12,104	23,063
Final Draft Screenplay	8,068	15,375
G. Rewrite of Screenplay	10,086	15,375
H. Polish of Screenplay	5,045	7,687

Low Budget—Photoplay costing less than $2,500,000

High Budget—Photoplay costing $2,500,000 or more

+ The MBA provides for a discount with respect to employment on a flat deal basis of a writer who has not been previously employed in television, theatrical films or dramatic radio, subject to an adjustment to full minimum if a photoplay is produced utilizing such writer's material. For details, contact the Guild.

WGA 1988 Theatrical and Television Basic Agreement
Television Compensation

Comedy-Variety Programs

Applicable Program Minimums

Length or Time Bracket	Effective 8/8/88– 8/31/89	Effective 9/1/89– 2/28/91	Effective 3/1/91– 5/1/92
5 minutes	$ 819	$ 860/856	$ 899/894/890
10 minutes	1,628	1,709/1,701	1,786/1,778/1,769
15 minutes	2,298	2,413/2,401	2,522/2,510/2,497
30 minutes	4,988	5,237/5,212	5,473/5,446/5,420
45 minutes	5,411	5,682/5,654	5,938/5,908/5,880
60 minutes	6,861	7,204/7,170	7,528/7,492/7,457
75 minutes	7,987	8,386/8,346	8,763/8,722/8,680
90 minutes	9,352	9,820/9,773	10,262/10,213/10,164

One Program Per Week,
Minimum Variety Show Commitment

If *all* writers on a once-per-week variety series are employed under a contract providing for guaranteed employment in cycles of thirteen (13) or more weeks, the applicable weekly minimum for each such writer is:

Effective	
8/8/88–8/31/89	$1,811
9/1/89–2/28/91	1,902/1,892
3/1/91–5/1/92	1,988/1,978/1,968

and the aggregate minimum compensation for each program is:

Number of Writers	Percentage of Applicable Program Minimums
1	100%
2	150%
3	175%
4	200%

plus 25% for each additional writer.

WGA 1988 Theatrical and Television Basic Agreement
Television Compensation

Network Prime Time

Length of Program: 15 minutes or less

	Effective 8/8/88– 8/31/89	Effective 9/1/89– 2/28/91	Effective 3/1/91– 5/1/92
Applicable Minimums			
Story +	$ 2,214	$ 2,325/2,314	$ 2,430/2,418/2,407
Teleplay	5,377	5,646/5,619	5,900/5,872/5,844

Installments:

+First Draft: 60% of Agreed Compensation but not less than 90% of minimum

Final Draft: Balance of Agreed Compensation

Story & Teleplay	6,652	6,985/6,951	7,299/7,264/7,229

Installments:

+Story: 30% of Agreed Compensation

First Draft Teleplay: 40% of Agreed Compensation or the difference between the Story Installment and 90% of minimum, whichever is greater

Final Draft Teleplay: Balance of Agreed Compensation

Length of Program: 30 minutes or less (but more than 15 minutes)

Story +	$ 4,058	$ 4,261/4,241	$ 4,453/4,432/4,411
Teleplay	8,733	9,170/9,126	9,583/9,537/9,491

Installments:

+First Draft: 60% of Agreed Compensation but not less than 90% of minimum

Final Draft: Balance of Agreed Compensation

Story & Teleplay	12,176	12,785/12,724	13,360/13,296/13,233

Installments:

+Story: 30% of Agreed Compensation

First Draft Teleplay: 40% of Agreed Compensation or the difference between the Story Installment and 90% of minimum, whichever is greater

Final Draft Teleplay: Balance of Agreed Compensation

WGA 1988 Theatrical and Television Basic Agreement
Television Compensation (continued)

Network Prime Time

Length of Program: 45 minutes or less (but more than 30 minutes)

Applicable Minimums	Effective 8/8/88– 8/31/89	Effective 9/1/89– 2/28/91	Effective 3/1/91– 5/1/92
Story +	$ 5,600	$ 5,880/5,852	$ 6,145/6,115/6,086
Teleplay	9,235	9,697/9,651	10,133/10,085/10,037
Installments:			
+First Draft:	60% of Agreed Compensation but not less than 90% of minimum		
Final Draft:	Balance of Agreed Compensation		
Story & Teleplay	14,034	14,736/14,666	15,399/15,326/15,253
Installments:			
+Story:	30% of Agreed Compensation		
First Draft Teleplay:	40% of Agreed Compensation or the difference between the Story Installment and 90% of minimum, whichever is greater		
Final Draft Teleplay:	Balance of Agreed Compensation		

Length of Program: 60 minutes or less (but more than 45 minutes)

	Effective 8/8/88– 8/31/89	Effective 9/1/89– 2/28/91	Effective 3/1/91– 5/1/92
Story +	$ 7,144	$ 7,501/7,465	$ 7,839/7,801/7,764
Teleplay	11,780	12,369/12,310	12,926/12,864/12,802
Installments:			
+First Draft:	60% of Agreed Compensation but not less than 90% of minimum		
Final Draft:	Balance of Agreed Compensation		
Story & Teleplay	17,906	18,801/18,712	19,647/19,554/19,460
Installments:			
+Story:	30% of Agreed Compensation		
First Draft Teleplay:	40% of Agreed Compensation or the difference between the Story Installment and 90% of minimum, whichever is greater		
Final Draft Teleplay:	Balance of Agreed Compensation		

+On pilots only, the writer is to be paid 10% of the first installment (as an advance against such first installment) upon commencement of services. The applicable minimum for a pilot story or story and teleplay is 150% of the applicable minimum set forth above.

Chapter 12
Syndication Contracts

Richard S. Newcombe

National syndicates that invest money in promoting and selling a previously unknown columnist naturally want to protect their investment. Columnists, on the other hand, want ownership of their own material and the freedom from what they consider burdensome provisions in their contract. The owner of Creators Syndicate offers you ten suggestions on:
   1. Clauses in syndication contracts and what they mean.
   2. Advice on what to avoid and negotiate.
   3. What is the syndicate's job.
   4. What is the columnist's job.

There are ten major syndicates in the United States. Most are owned by giant media companies. Their contracts contain as many differences as similarities. The syndicates and their owners are as follows:
   1. King Features Syndicate, Hearst Corporation
   2. United Media, Scripps-Howard
   3. Tribune Media Services, Tribune Company
   4. Universal Press Syndicate, Independent
   5. Los Angeles Times Syndicate, Times Mirror Company
   6. Creators Syndicate, Independent
   7. Washington Post Writers' Group, Washington Post Company
   8. New York Times Syndication Sales Corp., New York Times
   9. Copley News Service, Copley
   10. Chronicle Features, San Francisco Chronicle

Negotiating a Syndication Contract
   There are hundreds of smaller syndicates as well. Regardless of which syndicate you join, I'd like to offer ten specific suggestions for your syndication contract:
   1. Maintain ownership rights to your work.

2. Limit the term of the agreement to five years. At the end of the term, you should have the right of unconditional termination. You should be free to leave your syndicate—no strings attached.

3. Avoid any type of automatic renewal based on performance. If you are happy with the performance, then you should be free to exercise your option for renewal *voluntarily*. Most likely, you will perceive that it is in your best interest to renew the contract with your syndicate if your syndicate is working hard for you. But the choice should be yours. Many syndicates offer "five and five" or "ten and ten" contracts. These should be avoided. They mean the following: If the syndicate reaches certain sales quotas within the first five years of a "five and five" or within the first ten years of a "ten and ten," then your contract automatically renews for an additional five or ten years. From the viewpoint of the writer or artist, the problem is that if the syndicate fails to reach certain goals, the syndicate can cancel your feature at any time. In other words, a "ten and ten" means that you're stuck with the syndicate for twenty years if your feature succeeds, but you have no protection against the syndicate cancelling your feature at any time during those twenty years if your feature does not reach certain sales goals. I believe that a twenty-year personal service contract is excessive. So do several states, including California, which has a seven-year limit on personal service contracts.

4. Stay away from clauses that attempt to keep part of your future income if you switch syndicates.

5. Avoid clauses granting rights of first refusal and "topping privileges—this means you're stuck with one syndicate if it can top the financial offer of another syndicate. You may want to switch for reasons other than money. For instance, let's say that you sign a five-year contract with a clause stating that if you receive an offer from a competing syndicate at the end of the five years, your original syndicate has the right to top the offer. If they offer more money, then you're stuck. But what if you want to switch syndicates for reasons other than money? What if your editor switches syndicates, and you worked very well with that editor? What if the new editor does not appreciate or understand your work? The point is: Avoid contractual clauses that are aimed at limiting your freedom.

6. If you are an artist, insist upon keeping your original artwork.

7. Maintain creative control over all licensing and book agreements.

8. Avoid "exclusivity" clauses, which state that if you do a second, dissimilar feature, you are obligated to have it represented by your original syndicate. You might want to do the second feature with a competing syndicate in order to see which syndicate you prefer.

9. The standard syndicate agreement calls for a 50/50 split of the net proceeds from a new feature. I believe this is fair. A syndicate is neither a publishing company nor a talent agency. It is a little of both. Your syndicate should offer editorial suggestions to your work (but you should retain editorial control), your syndicate will print your work, transmit it by wire or mail it to subscribing papers, sell it to new markets, promote it with ads and sales kits, collect the money from your client papers, and then send you a royalty check each month. Also, make sure that you get a list of papers and their rates attached to your monthly check.

10. Don't hesitate to write other syndicated columnists in care of their syndicates for advice. You will be surprised by how knowledgeable most of them are about syndicate contracts and how helpful they can be.

I apologize if my ten suggestions sound excessively cautious (avoid this, stay away from that, maintain equality, etc., etc.).

But I speak from experience—the experience of having run some of the largest syndicates in the world.

I saw first-hand many of the clauses I have described. They were in the contracts of the writers and artists I represented. I tried hard to change them, but I was a manager and not an owner. It was not until I owned my own syndicate that I was able to guarantee contracts that allow the type of freedom that I describe in my ten suggestions.

Despite these contractual abuses, which are found less frequently in the contracts signed today than they were even two years ago, I believe that most syndicates overall do a good job for the talent they represent.

It is the syndicate's job to discover talent and to nurture that talent with helpful suggestions. It is also the syndicate's job to develop a market for a feature by persuading newspaper editors to run the feature and promote it.

Having said this, I am always a little shocked to hear a syndicate executive claim to have developed a feature.

That's your job. That is the responsibility, ultimately, of the writer or artist. And of course it is the writer or artist—not the syndicate—who in the final analysis should receive the credit for a successful feature.

Perhaps you are wondering why there are so many clauses to be avoided in a syndicate contract. You might be asking, "Is this an industry *not* to be trusted?"

The answer is no. In fact, nearly all syndicate executives are honorable men and women who work hard for the talent they represent.

Today, you rarely see syndicate ownership clauses, or the clauses which state that the syndicate owns your work "in perpetuity." If you do see them, run a hundred miles.

More likely, you will see the clauses that I describe in my ten suggestions, and if you follow my advice, assuming you develop a successful feature, then you will be in the strongest possible position: You will have the freedom to do what you want while all the major syndicates are courting you.

If your syndicate is working hard for you, my advice is to stay. But if your syndicate is not doing the job for you, my advice is to switch. Just make sure you have that option.

Chapter 13
Federal Taxes and the Writer

Patricia Fox Fleck

The Tax Reform Act of 1986 became law amid a flurry of debate and spawned countless cartoons of accountants and taxpayers trying to cope with the "simplified" rules. When you finally had it all figured out along came the 1988 Technical Tax Corrections Bill that gave writers back their old way of calculating their expenses and taxes. (Thanks to the many writers who gave of their time and talents lobbying in Washington.) This chapter, rewritten as many times as the tax laws for writers, includes:

1. The special considerations and requirements of the home office deduction including the new MACRS method of depreciation.

2. The reprieve writers have from the Tax Reform Act of 1986

3. Depreciation schedules for computers, cars, and office equipment.

4. What records you need to keep if your writing is, "once and done."

5. Why you might want to hang onto your rejection slips.

Whoever said there's nothing as constant as change must have been working for the IRS. Tax rules for freelance writers have been constantly changing since the first editions of this book, and the new changes are more complex than ever.

The number one rule, however, remains the same: If your freelance earnings exceed your expenses, regardless of the amount, they are subject to tax. And in most cases you must show a profit in three (formerly two) out of five consecutive years or be able to prove to the IRS you are writing to make a profit.

Deductions for Working at Home

It can be your garret, your cellar, your spare room, but to qualify as a deduction your home office must be used regularly and exclusively for writing. It can be the corner of a studio or loft apartment, but no other use can be made of the space. It must be your principal place of business. If you are a doctor, lawyer, teacher, etc. who also writes you can have a principal place of business for each job and still qualify for the home office deduction for your writing (as long as you are writing for profit).

Example: If you rent a five-room apartment for $300 a month (lucky you) and use one room exclusively for writing, you are entitled to deduct one fifth of the rent, which comes to $60 a month or $720 a year. Add to this one fifth of your utilities. If you own your own home and use one room for writing, you can deduct the allocated expenses of operating that room. Among expenses allowed are interest on mortgage, real estate taxes, repairs, cost of utilities, home insurance premiums, and depreciation on the room.

If you used the room prior to 1987, you continue to use the Accelerated Cost Recovery System (ACRS) over fifteen, eighteen, or nineteen years depending on when you placed the building in service.

The easiest method of calculating the depreciation deduction is the straight line method, which is simply dividing the total cost of the property by the statutory number of years (depending upon when you placed the building in service).

Note: If you use the accelerated method as opposed to straight line, all depreciation taken may be subject to tax as ordinary income when you sell the property. It is generally advantageous to use the more conservative straight line method.

Beginning January 1, 1987 a new method of depreciation known as the Modified Accelerated Cost Recovery System (MACRS) replaced ACRS. For buildings the depreciation must be taken over thirty-one and one-half years straight line.

A Limit to the Home-Office Deduction

The new law allows home office deductions only to the extent of "net income" which is gross income minus all other deductible expenses *other than* the home office.

Example: If you made $5,000 gross income from the sale of magazine articles and had $4,000 deductible expenses such as paper, books for research, postage, etc. you'd have a net income of $1,000, which is the maximum amount of home-office expense you could deduct. If your deductible expenses exceeded the $5,000 gross income you would not be able to claim any deduction for your home office other than expenses such as property taxes and home mortgage interest that are deductible without regard to business.

Home office expenses not able to be claimed in a given year can be carried forward and used in a future year, but are subject to "net income" limitations.

Writing Off Operating Expenses

After a long and bitter struggle against the footnote to the 1986 Tax Reform Act, the 1988 Technical Tax Corrections bill returned to authors their previous tax status. This means that the expenses CAN be deducted in the year that they were incurred. Example: If a writer received a $20,000 advance for a book and racks up $3,000 that year in expenses, the writer can deduct the entire $3,000 in that year.

Note: Authors who capitalized their 1987 expenses under the "safe harbor three year rule" may file an amended return for 1987 OR may continue to capitalize their 1987 expenses over 1988 and 1989, but resume current deduction for expenses in 1988.

Deducting a Computer

The days of parchment and quill pen are over. In many cases the days of a typewriter and ream of paper are too. Today many of us need computers, printers, and three kinds of software to get the work out and earn income. If you buy a computer and use it more than 50 percent of the time for writing, you can write off the costs over six years, 52 percent being written off in the first two years because the new law uses a formula that provides a bigger initial write-off.

Other Equipment

All other office equipment (typewriters, photocopiers, furniture, etc.) is now considered seven-year recovery property.

In lieu of taking depreciation you may elect to expense up to $10,000 per year of MACRS personal property. Instead of taking depreciation as outlined above, you can deduct the cost of qualified equipment and furniture up to $10,000. You may not deduct more than your net income.

Depreciation

Percentage of cost written off each year.

Computers

Year 1	20%
Year 2	32%
Year 3	19.20%
Year 4	11.52%
Year 5	11.52%
Year 6	5.76%
	100.00%

**Other Office
Equipment**

Year 1	14.29%
Year 2	24.49%
Year 3	17.49%
Year 4	12.49%
Year 5	8.93%
Year 6	8.92%
Year 7	8.93%
Year 8	4.46%
	100.00%

Once-and-Done Publishing

If your income is from writing materials that are published once and done (articles, short stories, etc.), the following will serve as guidelines for keeping records to get your deductions.

Receipts. Keep them for everything related to your writing—books, office supplies, magazine subscriptions, postage.

Records. Keep good records. Pay bills by check and enter all expenses and sales in a ledger (it's also deductible!). If you keep your records hit or miss, the IRS will hit hard and you'll miss savings on taxes.

What's Deductible

All writing supplies including paper, photocopying, pens, envelopes, and ribbons are deductible. So are repairs and maintenance of writing equipment, including your computer, typewriter, tape recorder, camera, and so forth.

Courses and conferences you attend to increase your professional capabilities can be deducted, but not those you take to *become* a writer. The IRS rule is that courses must be "refresher" or improve you professionally to be deductible. Besides deducting these you can deduct your mileage (details below), 100 percent of cost of public transportation, and lodging. Meals and/or entertainment are presently only 80 percent deductible. Receipts must be kept.

Car Expense

Take 22½ cents a mile for the first 15,000 miles you travel on writing-related missions and 11 cents a mile over 15,000. Accurate mileage records must be kept in writing. If you don't take the 22½ cents a mile, you can take the actual expense of operating your car: gas, oil, tires, maintenance, and depreciation (check instructions on new depreciation). If you use your car more than 50 percent for business you can write off that portion of the car's cost attributable to business on a five-year schedule, compared to three years under the old law. Actually it will take six years to write off the cost because you only get a half year's worth of write-offs the first year you put the car in service, so the remainder carries over to the sixth year.

Luxury Cars
If your car costs more than $12,800 the deductions are further limited, because your car is classified a "luxury car," and you will have a slower depreciation schedule. While you can still write off all costs, it will take longer to do, as shown in the table.

Car Depreciation Write-offs for Business
Cars Costing Less Than $12,800

Year 1	20%
Year 2	32%
Year 3	19.20%
Year 4	11.52%
Year 5	11.52%
Year 6	5.76%
	100.00%

Cars Costing More Than $12,800

Year 1	$2,560
Year 2	$4,100
Year 3	$2,450
Year 4	$1,475
Subsequent Years	$1,475

Social Security Tax
If you earn $400 or more after deductions you are required to pay Social Security tax, and you must fill out a Schedule SE (self-employment) with your tax return. (See Chapter Fourteen on Social Security.)

Estimated Tax Payments
If you expect your estimated tax will be $500 or more you are required to file an estimated tax return on Form 1040 ES. The return, with one fourth the expected tax, is due April 15 of the year the income is earned. Additional quarterly installments are due June 15 and September 15; the final installment is due January 15 of the following year.

Tax Forms You Should Know
Many of us file Form 1040 joint return with spouse. As writers we also file a Schedule C (profit or loss) from Business or Profession, a

Schedule SE for Social Security, a Form 4562 for depreciation, and often Schedules A and B (for itemized deductions, dividends, and interest income).

Read these forms carefully: A reading will show you how to provide the information asked for and the advantages of doing so.

Evidence to Keep

Rejection slips: Keep them. When the subject of rejection slips comes up at writers' conferences, the instructors generally frown and tell you to throw them away. Be done with them, they advise.

Not me. I advise you to store the slips and postmarked envelopes in a folder, carton, or spare room—someplace you won't have to look at them, but where they are accessible should you be the featured guest at a tax audit. What better way to establish you're a working writer than to hit the IRS agent (not physically) with an avalanche of rejection slips and other correspondence with publishers?

Encouraging letters? Hold on to them too, for heaven's sake, in a place where you can see them when the writing gets rough. And have your ledger, receipts, and cancelled checks ready. Audits, like toothaches, sometimes happen to the best of us.

One Final Note

Examples used here are for guides only. Different requirements are made of writers in different circumstances. For any long-term writing projects, such as novels or histories that may take more than a year to complete are subject to the new capitalization laws. Remember, laws keep changing, be sure to have the latest IRS forms and instruction booklets.

When you keep accurate records throughout the year, save receipts and pay by check, preparing for your April 15 deadline won't be so bad. (They made me say that!)

Review/Chapter 13

The number one rule for freelance writers: If your earnings exceed your expenses, you are subject to tax.

Your home office, in order to qualify for deduction must:

✓be used exclusively for writing

✓must be your principal place of business

Expenses incurred during a long-term project are written off in the same year as they occur.

What's deductible?

✓all writing supplies

✓repairs and maintenance of equipment

✔courses and conferences to increase your professional capabilities
✔mileage
✔public transportation and lodging
✔80% of meals and entertainment

If you earn $400 or more after deductions you are required to pay Social Security Tax.

If you expect to owe taxes of $500 or more you are required to file an estimated tax return.

Keep accurate records.

SCHEDULE C
(Form 1040)

Department of the Treasury
Internal Revenue Service

Profit or (Loss) From Business or Profession
(Sole Proprietorship)

Partnerships, Joint Ventures, etc., Must File Form 1065.

▶ Attach to Form 1040, Form 1041, or Form 1041S.   ▶ See Instructions for Schedule C (Form 1040).

OMB No. 1545-0074

1987

Attachment Sequence No. **09**

Name of proprietor: Deidre Stephens

Social security number (SSN): 268 : 44 : 3245

A Principal business or profession, including product or service (see Instructions): freelance writer

B Principal business code (from Part IV) ▶ 8 8 8 8

C Business name and address ▶ 1121 Lehigh Street, Easton, PA

D Employer ID number (Not SSN)

E Method(s) used to value closing inventory:
- (1) ☐ Cost
- (2) ☐ Lower of cost or market
- (3) ☐ Other (attach explanation)

			Yes	No
F	Accounting method: (1) ☒ Cash (2) ☐ Accrual (3) ☐ Other (specify) ▶			
G	Was there any change in determining quantities, costs, or valuations between opening and closing inventory? (If "Yes," attach explanation.)			x
H	Are you deducting expenses for an office in your home?		x	
I	Did you file **Form 941** for this business for any quarter in 1987?			x
J	Did you "materially participate" in the operation of this business during 1987? (If "No," see Instructions for limitations on losses.)		x	
K	Was this business in operation at the end of 1987?		x	
L	How many months was this business in operation during 1987? ▶	12		

M If this schedule includes a loss, credit, deduction, income, or other tax benefit relating to a tax shelter required to be registered, check here. ▶ ☐
If you check this box, you **MUST** attach **Form 8271**.

Part I   Income

1a	Gross receipts or sales	1a	2,900 00
b	Less: Returns and allowances	1b	
c	Subtract line 1b from line 1a and enter the balance here	1c	2,900 00
2	Cost of goods sold and/or operations (from Part III, line 8)	2	
3	Subtract line 2 from line 1c and enter the **gross profit** here	3	
4	Other income (including windfall profit tax credit or refund received in 1987)	4	
5	Add lines 3 and 4. This is the **gross income** ▶	5	2,900 00

Part II   Deductions

6	Advertising			23	Repairs	
7	Bad debts from sales or services (see Instructions)			24	Supplies (not included in Part III)	
8	Bank service charges			25	Taxes	
9	Car and truck expenses	50	94	26	Travel, meals, and entertainment:	
10	Commissions			a	Travel	
11	Depletion			b	Total meals and entertainment	49 95
12	Depreciation and section 179 deduction from Form 4562 (not included in Part III)	709	70	c	Enter 20% of line 26b subject to limitations (see Instructions)	10 00
13	Dues and publications	103	50	d	Subtract line 26c from 26b	39 95
14	Employee benefit programs			27	Utilities and telephone	52 33
15	Freight (not included in Part III)			28a	Wages	
16	Insurance			b	Jobs credit	
17	Interest:			c	Subtract line 28b from 28a	
a	Mortgage (paid to financial institutions)			29	Other expenses (list type and amount):	
b	Other	28	68		allocated home	
18	Laundry and cleaning				office expenses	
19	Legal and professional services				(see schedule	
20	Office expense	175	59		attached)	1,387 00
21	Pension and profit-sharing plans					
22	Rent on business property					

30	Add amounts in columns for lines 6 through 29. These are the **total deductions** ▶	30	2,547 69
31	Net profit or (loss). Subtract line 30 from line 5. If a profit, enter here and on Form 1040, line 13, and on Schedule SE, line 2 (or line 5 of Form 1041 or Form 1041S). If a loss, you **MUST** go on to line 32	31	352 31

32 If you have a loss, you **MUST** answer this question: "Do you have amounts for which you are not at risk in this business?" (See Instructions.) ☐ Yes ☐ No
If "Yes," you **MUST** attach **Form 6198.** If "No," enter the loss on Form 1040, line 13, and on Schedule SE, line 2 (or line 5 of Form 1041 or Form 1041S).

Chapter 14
Social Security and the Self-Employed Writer

Louise Boggess

Social Security seems a long way off to most of us. We usually only think about it when we file (and pay) our form SE with our tax returns, but there are some facts self-employed writers need to know about Social Security. This chapter covers:

1. How you qualify for Social Security. How to determine if you qualify as self-employed, and how to use the "optional method."

2. Understanding the "quarter" system and how to make sure you qualify.

3. How to obtain a statement of your earnings record.

4. Determining your benefits for full or partial retirement.

5. How other family members can qualify for benefits.

6. How to apply for any and all benefits due you and how the appeals process works.

As a self-employed writer you can qualify for Social Security and receive a monthly income for yourself and your family when you retire or become disabled. When you die, your survivors may qualify for payments. Because Social Security protects the family from loss of income, the married writer obviously receives more extensive protection from these programs than the single one. To receive these benefits, however, you must establish earnings credit based on your qualifying income.

Qualifying for Social Security

To determine your qualifying income, include money earned from writing as well as related activities. Many self-employed writers supplement their literary income by personal appearances, lectures, or manuscript criticism. As long as these relate to your writing, you count them as qualifying income.

If you instruct a class in writing through a school or college, you normally become an employee. To count fees from teaching writing classes as self-employment income, *you* must organize the class and pay the operating costs. Some schools and colleges, however, do employ writers as part-time instructors and pay them as independent consultants and not as employees.

Social Security will recognize you as an independent consultant or self-employed person when you establish such a status in your community through membership in professional writers' organizations, publishing credits, and other business activities. In such a case, you request the school or college to pay you as self-employed and count such earnings as qualifying income.

In 1951, Congress required self-employed writers who sold their literary work for a profit and who earned a net income of $400 or more a year to contribute to Social Security programs. *Net income* consists of gross income minus allowable business deductions.

A one-time sale of a book, article, or short story does not necessarily qualify you as a self-employed writer even though you receive a large amount of money. You must write consistently over a period of time. As long as you earn a net of $400 or more, year after year, you write consistently. Although a majority of writers unquestionably qualify as self-employed, many borderline cases do exist. Social Security decides these instances on an individual basis.

The Optional Method

Even though you do not earn a net of $400, you may use an optional method of reporting your income to build up your earnings credit and qualify for the insurance programs. You can choose this method when your actual net earnings add up to $400 or more in at least two of the three previous years. The law limits your use of the optional plan to five times and then only if your net earnings amount to less than two thirds of your gross income. Do not report earnings less than $400 on Schedule SE for the Internal Revenue Service, but report the optional method earnings instead.

According to the optional method, if your gross income varies between $600 and $2,400, you may report either two thirds of your gross or your actual net earnings if $400 or more. If your gross income amounts to $2,400 or more and the actual net earnings $1,600 or less, you report either $1,600 or your actual net earnings to the IRS.

The law requires that you report all net income up to a stated maximum set at the end of the year and based on the increase in average wages. The maximum for 1988 amounted to $45,000. When you coauthor with your spouse or with your son or daughter, each of you reports the earned incomes allotted to you toward this maximum.

You may work as an employee and as self-employed. In this event you report your earnings toward the maximum first as an employee. If your earnings amount to less than the maximum set by Social

Social Security Self-Employment Tax

▶ See Instructions for Schedule SE (Form 1040).
▶ Attach to Form 1040.

OMB No. 1545-0074

1988

Attachment
Sequence No. 18

Name of person with **self-employment** income (as shown on social security card)	Social security number of person with **self-employment** income ▶		

Who Must File Schedule SE

You must file Schedule SE if:

- Your net earnings from self-employment were $400 or more (or you had wages of $100 or more from an electing church or church organization); AND

- You did not have wages (subject to social security or railroad retirement tax) of $45,000 or more.

For more information about Schedule SE, see the Instructions.

Note: *Most taxpayers can now use the new short Schedule SE on this page. But, you may have to use the longer Schedule SE that is on the back.*

Who MUST Use the Long Schedule SE (Section B)

You must use Section B if ANY of the following applies:

- You choose the "optional method" to figure your self-employment tax. See Section B, Part II;

- You are a minister, member of a religious order, or Christian Science practitioner and received IRS approval (from **Form 4361**) not to be taxed on your earnings from these sources, but you owe self-employment tax on other earnings;

- You are an employee of a church or church organization that chose by law not to pay employer social security taxes;

- You have tip income that is subject to social security tax, but you did not report those tips to your employer; OR

- You are a government employee with wages subject ONLY to the 1.45% medicare part of the social security tax.

Section A—Short Schedule SE

(Read above to see if you must use the long Schedule SE on the back (Section B).)

1	Net farm profit or (loss) from Schedule F (Form 1040), line 39, and farm partnerships, Schedule K-1 (Form 1065), line 14a	**1**		
2	Net profit or (loss) from Schedule C (Form 1040), line 31, and Schedule K-1 (Form 1065), line 14a (other than farming). See the Instructions for other income to report	**2**		
3	Add lines 1 and 2. Enter the total. If the total is less than $400, **do not** file this schedule	**3**		
4	The largest amount of combined wages and self-employment earnings subject to social security or railroad retirement tax (tier 1) for 1988 is	**4**	$45,000	00
5	Total social security wages and tips from Forms W-2 and railroad retirement compensation (tier 1) . . .	**5**		
6	Subtract line 5 from line 4. Enter the result. (If the result is zero or less, **do not** file this schedule.) . . .	**6**		
7	Enter the **smaller** of line 3 or line 6	**7**		
	If line 7 is $45,000, enter $5,859 on line 8. Otherwise, multiply line 7 by .1302 and enter the result on line 8		×.1302	
8	Self-employment tax. Enter this amount on Form 1040, line 48	**8**		

For Paperwork Reduction Act Notice, see Form 1040 Instructions.   Schedule SE (Form 1040) 1988

Name of person with **self-employment** income (as shown on social security card)	Social security number of person with **self-employment** income ▶

Section B—Long Schedule SE

(Before completing, see if you can use the short Schedule SE on the other side (Section A).)

A   If your only self-employment income was from earnings as a minister, member of a religious order, or Christian Science practitioner, AND you filed **Form 4361**, then DO NOT file Schedule SE. Instead, write "Exempt-Form 4361" on Form 1040, line 48. However, if you filed Form 4361, but have $400 or more of other earnings subject to self-employment tax, continue with Part I and check here.   ▶ ☐

B   If your only earnings subject to self-employment tax are wages from an electing church or church-controlled organization that is exempt from employer social security taxes and you are not a minister or a member of a religious order, skip lines 1–3b. Enter zero on line 3c and go on to line 5a.

Part I   Figure Social Security Self-Employment Tax

1	Net farm profit or (loss) from Schedule F (Form 1040), line 39, and farm partnerships, Schedule K-1 (Form 1065), line 14a	**1**	
2	Net profit or (loss) from Schedule C (Form 1040), line 31, and Schedule K-1 (Form 1065), line 14a (other than farming). (See Instructions for other income to report.) Employees of an electing church or church-controlled organization **do not** enter your Form W-2 wages on line 2. See the Instructions	**2**	
3a	Enter the amount from line 1 (**or**, if you elected the farm optional method, Part II, line 10)	**3a**	
b	Enter the amount from line 2 (**or**, if you elected the nonfarm optional method, Part II, line 12)	**3b**	
c	Add lines 3a and 3b. Enter the total. If the total is less than $400, **do not** file this schedule. **(Exception:** If you are an employee of an electing church or church-controlled organization and the total of lines 3a and 3b is less than $400, enter zero and complete the rest of this schedule.)	**3c**	
4	The largest amount of combined wages and self-employment earnings subject to social security or railroad retirement tax (tier 1) for 1988 is	**4**	$45,000 00

5a	Total social security wages and tips from Forms W-2 and railroad retirement compensation (tier 1). **Note:** Government employees whose wages are subject only to the 1.45% medicare tax and employees of certain church or church-controlled organizations should **not** include those wages on this line. See Instructions **5a**		
b	Unreported tips subject to social security tax from Form 4137, line 9, or to railroad retirement tax (tier 1). **5b**		
c	Add lines 5a and 5b. Enter the total	**5c**	
6a	Subtract line 5c from line 4. Enter the result. (If the result is zero or less, enter zero.)	**6a**	
b	Enter your medicare qualified government wages if you are required to use the worksheet in the Instructions **6b**		
c	Enter your Form W-2 wages of $100 or more from an electing church or church-controlled organization **6c**		
d	Add lines 3c and 6c. Enter the total	**6d**	
7	Enter the **smaller** of line 6a or line 6d	**7**	
	If line 7 is $45,000, enter $5,859 on line 8. Otherwise, multiply line 7 by .1302 and enter the result on line 8		× .1302
8	Self-employment tax. Enter this amount on Form 1040, line 48	**8**	

Part II   Optional Method To Figure Net Earnings (See "Who Can File Schedule SE" in the Instructions.)

See Instructions for limitations. Generally, you may use this part **only** if:

A   Your **gross** farm income[1] was not more than $2,400; **or**

B   Your **gross** farm income[1] was more than $2,400 and your **net** farm profits[2] were **less** than $1,600; **or**

C   Your **net** nonfarm profits[3] were less than $1,600 and also **less** than two-thirds (⅔) of your **gross** nonfarm income.[4]

Note: If line 2 above is two-thirds (⅔) or more of your gross nonfarm income[4], or if line 2 is $1,600 or more, you may **not** use the optional method.

[1] From Schedule F (Form 1040), line 12, and Schedule K-1 (Form 1065), line 14b.   [3] From Schedule C (Form 1040), line 31, and Schedule K-1 (Form 1065), line 14a.
[2] From Schedule F (Form 1040), line 39, and Schedule K-1 (Form 1065), line 14a.   [4] From Schedule C (Form 1040), line 5, and Schedule K-1 (Form 1065), line 14c.

9	Maximum income for optional methods	**9**	$1,600 00
10	**Farm Optional Method**—If you meet test A or B above, enter the **smaller** of: two-thirds (⅔) of gross farm income from Schedule F (Form 1040), line 12, and farm partnerships, Schedule K-1 (Form 1065), line 14b; **or** $1,600. Also enter this amount on line 3a above	**10**	
11	Subtract line 10 from line 9. Enter the result	**11**	
12	**Nonfarm Optional Method**—If you meet test C above, enter the **smallest** of: two-thirds (⅔) of gross nonfarm income from Schedule C (Form 1040), line 5, and Schedule K-1 (Form 1065), line 14c (other than farming); **or** $1,600; **or**, if you elected the farm optional method, the amount on line 11. Also enter this amount on line 3b above	**12**	

For Paperwork Reduction Act Notice, see Form 1040 Instructions.   Schedule SE (Form 1040) 1988

Security as taxable, you then use your net earnings as a writer to qualify for the full amount.

You report your self-employment earnings and the amount of your tax by April 15 of each year on the Internal Revenue Service form Schedule SE (Computation of Social Security Self-Employment Tax).

Even though you do not owe any income tax, you must complete Form 1040 and Schedule SE to pay self-employment Social Security tax. You report even if you already receive Social Security benefits.

Self-Employment Tax

The self-employed writer pays his or her entire tax. The employer pays half of the employee's tax on total earnings up to the maximum, but as a self-employed writer you pay only on your net earnings. In 1988, based on the Social Security law, the tax rate on self-employment income increased to 15.02 percent to equal the combined employee-employer rates. In 1988 and 1989 the law also provided credits against liability of 2.0 percent. After 1989 special deduction provisions designed to treat the self-employed in much the same manner as employees-employers will replace the credit. The table shows the tax rate, the credit, and the amount of tax paid.

Self-Employment Tax Rate

Year	Tax	Credit	Actual Tax
1988–1989	15.02%	2.0%	13.02%
1990 and after	15.30%		15.30%

Social Security records your covered earnings under your name and Social Security number. You should check your record every three years to make sure all your earnings get credited. Your earnings determine your qualifications for benefits and the amount of payment. If you want a statement of your earnings record, get a Form SSA 7004 from any Social Security office, fill out the form, add first-class postage, and mail it to the Social Security Administration. This form contains the essential information Social Security needs to check your record.

You will find the Social Security office listed under United States Government in your local telephone directory.

Getting Credits

Although you pay taxes on qualifying income, you will not receive any Social Security benefits until you have attained an insured status. You acquire an insured status by contributing to a certain number of "quarters." The self-employed writer earns a quarter of coverage for each $470 of net earnings for an annual net income of $1,880 or

SOCIAL SECURITY ADMINISTRATION

Request for Earnings and Benefit Estimate Statement

To receive a free statement of your earnings covered by Social Security and your estimated future benefits, all you need to do is fill out this form. Please print or type your answers. When you have completed the form, fold it and mail it to us.

1. Name shown on your Social Security card:

   First ▢▢▢▢ Middle Initial ▢ Last ▢▢▢▢

2. Your Social Security number as shown on your card:

   ▢▢▢ - ▢▢ - ▢▢▢▢

3. Your date of birth:

   Month ▢▢ Day ▢▢ Year ▢▢

4. Other Social Security numbers you may have used:

   ▢▢▢ - ▢▢ - ▢▢▢▢
   ▢▢▢ - ▢▢ - ▢▢▢▢

5. Your Sex: ▢ Male ▢ Female

6. Other names you have used (including a maiden name):

7. Show your actual earnings for last year and your estimated earnings for this year. Include only wages and/or net self-employment income subject to Social Security tax.

   A. Last year's actual earnings:

   $ ▢▢▢ , ▢▢▢ . 0 0
   Dollars only

   B. This year's estimated earnings:

   $ ▢▢▢ , ▢▢▢ . 0 0
   Dollars only

8. Show the age at which you plan to retire: _____

9. Below, show an amount which you think best represents your future average yearly earnings between now and when you plan to retire. The amount should be a yearly average, not your total future lifetime earnings. Only show earnings subject to Social Security tax.

   Most people should enter the same amount as this year's estimated earnings (the amount shown in 7B). The reason for this is that we will show your retirement benefit estimate in today's dollars, but adjusted to account for average wage growth in the national economy.

   However, if you expect to earn significantly more or less in the future than what you currently earn because of promotions, a job change, part-time work, or an absence from the work force, enter the amount in today's dollars that will most closely reflect your future average yearly earnings. Do not add in cost-of-living, performance, or scheduled pay increases or bonuses.

   Your future average yearly earnings:

   $ ▢▢▢ , ▢▢▢ . 0 0
   Dollars only

10. Address where you want us to send the statement:

    Name

    Street Address (Include Apt. No., P.O. Box, or Rural Route)

    City   State   Zip Code

I am asking for information about my own Social Security record or the record of a person I am authorized to represent. I understand that if I deliberately request information under false pretenses I may be guilty of a federal crime and could be fined and/or imprisoned. I authorize you to send the statement of my earnings and benefit estimates to me or my representative through a contractor.

Please sign your name (Do not print).

▶ _____

Date _____ (Area Code) Daytime Telephone No. _____

ABOUT THE PRIVACY ACT

Social Security is allowed to collect the facts on this form under Section 205 of the Social Security Act. We need them to quickly identify your record and prepare the earnings statement you asked us for. Giving us these facts is voluntary. However, without them we may not be able to give you an earnings and benefit estimate statement. Neither the Social Security Administration nor its contractor will use the information for any other purpose.

SP ▢

Form SSA-7004-PC-OP1 (6/88) DESTROY PRIOR EDITIONS

Moisten, fold, and seal before mailing.

more. No one receives credit for more than four quarters a year no matter how much he or she earns. The amount of earnings required for a quarter increases automatically in future years as average wages rise.

If you will reach age 62 in 1991 or later, you will become fully insured for life when you have credit for ten years or forty quarters of coverage. (Those reaching 62 earlier need fewer credits.) If you formerly worked as an employee, these earned quarters as well as the self-employed ones count toward your insured status. Fortunately, you need not earn these quarters consecutively. You may receive benefits for retirement, disability, and survivor's insurance with less than ten years' credit, as explained later.

If you stop writing before you earn enough credit, you do not qualify for benefits. The credit you earn stays on your record, and you can add to it by returning to writing and paying taxes on your income. As a self-employed writer, you continue to pay taxes as long as you earn a net of $400 or more, even after retirement.

Year of Birth	Normal Retirement Age[1]
1937 or earlier	65
1938	65 and 2 months
1939	65 and 4 months
1940	65 and 6 months
1941	65 and 8 months
1942	65 and 10 months
1943–1954	66
1955	66 and 2 months
1956	66 and 4 months
1957	66 and 6 months
1958	66 and 8 months
1959	66 and 10 months
1960 and later	67

[1]Normal retirement age is the earliest age at which unreduced retirement benefits can be received.

When You Can Receive Retirement Benefits

Congress never intended old-age insurance as your total income for retirement at age sixty-two to sixty-five. Rather, it viewed Social Security payments as a basis upon which to plan full retirement.

The normal retirement age today is sixty-five. Starting in the year 2000, the age at which full benefits are payable will increase in gradual steps until it reaches sixty-seven. This will affect people born in 1938 and later. Reduced benefits will still be payable at sixty-two, but the reduction will be larger than it is now. The chart shown here gives the Social Security normal retirement age by year of birth.

Partial Retirement

Today you need not retire entirely at sixty-five but can continue to work and increase your income as long as you do not earn more than $8,400 at ages sixty-five through sixty-nine or $6,120 for those under sixty-five. When your earnings exceed the limit, Social Security withholds $1 in benefits for each $2 you earn over the allowed amount. The exempt amounts will increase in future years to keep pace with average wages.

If you return to work after receiving retirement benefits or delay retirement until you reach seventy, you will receive an extra amount in payments. The amount varies according to your year of birth from 1 percent to 8 percent. For those who became sixty-five in 1989, the benefit increases 3 percent for each year (¼ of 1 percent for each month) you delay retirement. Starting for people who reach sixty-five in 1990 and later, the credit will gradually increase until it reaches 8 percent in 2009. You may secure reduced benefits at sixty-two, but the reduction becomes much larger than at present.

In figuring your income for this earnings test, do not count royalties from books sold before you retired at sixty-five; however, you must include them in your net earnings for the Social Security tax. When you retire before age sixty-five, your royalties count in the earnings test. The earnings test also applies to dependents drawing Social Security payments; it no longer applies when you reach seventy.

Social Security provides a grace year. During the first year of retirement, any month you earn less than $700 between ages sixty-five and sixty-nine and $510 if under sixty-five, you can still collect full benefits. Social Security pays full retirement even though your total income exceeds the annual limit.

In 1984, Congress placed two other limitations on your retirement pay. First, if you or your spouse receive a railroad, federal, state, or local government pension, the dependent's check gets reduced $2 for each $3 of the amount of the pension. For more details get the leaflet, "Government Pension Offset, Fact Sheet No. 1" from the Social Security office.

Secondly, you will pay federal income tax on up to half of your Social Security payment when your total income exceeds $32,000 for a couple filing jointly; $25,000 for an individual. (A different rule applies to a couple filing separately.) Social Security deducts the payment for health insurance from the monthly amount you receive. To determine your Social Security payment, you must include these deductions for health insurance.

The amount of your benefits subjected to tax equals the smaller of
- One half of your benefits, or
- One half of the amount by which your adjusted gross income, plus tax-exempt interest, plus one half of your Social Security benefits that will exceed the set limit.

You will receive a form from Social Security showing the total amount of benefits you receive during the year and so will the Internal Revenue Service.

Contact the Social Security office if you have any questions about your benefit amount and ask the Internal Revenue Service on how to figure your taxable income.

Other Family Members Can Qualify

In addition to the retiree, other family members can also qualify for benefits. (Child refers to a natural, legally adopted, or stepchild.)

1. A spouse sixty-two or older.
2. Unmarried children under eighteen (or under nineteen if full-time high school student).
3. Unmarried children eighteen or over who became severely disabled before age twenty-two.
4. A spouse under sixty-two who cares for children under sixteen or disabled who receives benefits based on the retiree's earnings.
5. A divorced spouse sixty-two or over if the marriage lasted ten years or more.

Beginning in January 1985, a divorced spouse whose marriage lasted ten years or more (age sixty-two) who secured a divorce at least two years previously may get benefits even if the qualified person has not applied for retirement. When the parents become disabled or die, the child may qualify for benefits based on a grandparent's earnings. The grandparent must support the child.

You apply for retirement any time within three months before you reach sixty-two or sixty-five. By all means apply at least the last day of the month your benefits will start. Researching your records and determining your payment require time.

When you go to the Social Security office, take your card or number, a public birth certificate, marriage certificate, your children's public birth certificates if they receive benefits, and Schedule C of your federal income tax for two years or W-2 forms for two years. The booklet "Estimating Your Retirement Social Security Payment" explains how to determine the amount. You may secure disability benefits before you reach retirement age.

Disability

Disability insurance offers the writer under sixty-five the greatest protection. You're considered disabled if a severe physical or mental condition prevents you from engaging in "any substantial gainful work" for at least twelve months or is expected to result in death.

To qualify for disability, you must meet the following requirements in age and work credits:

1. Before age twenty-four: You need credit for one and one half years of work in the three-year period ending when your disability starts.
2. Age twenty-four through thirty-one: Credit for half the time between twenty-one and the time you became disabled.
3. Age thirty-one or older: You generally must have earned at least twenty credits in the ten years immediately before you become disabled. You also need to have as many total work credits as you would need for retirement. The following chart shows the amount of credits.

Born after 1929, become disabled at age	Born before 1930, become disabled before 62 in	Years of work credit you need
31 through 42		5
44		5½
46		6
48		6½
50		7
52	1981	7½
53	1982	7¾
54	1983	8
55	1984	8¼
56	1985	8½
58	1987	9
60	1989	9½
62 or older	1991 or later	10

An exception pertains to blindness. If you become blind, the required credits may have been earned at any time after 1936; you need no recent credit.

Eligibility for another government benefit can affect the amount of your disability payment. Payments from federal, state, or civil service, military, or worker's compensation cannot exceed 80 percent of your average current earnings before you became disabled.

A government pension offset may also reduce the Social Security payments of a widow, widower, or a spouse of a disabled worker as much as two thirds of the amount of the pension. Ask for the free fact sheet "Government Pension Offset" at any Social Security office. Your payment also becomes subject to Internal Revenue tax.

Do make application for disability as soon as you learn of your condition. If you cannot physically go to the office, you may send a spouse or relative. You or your relative should take your Social Security card or number; the names, addresses, and phone numbers of doctors, hospitals, clinics, and health institutions that treated you, along with the approximate dates; a work summary; your federal tax return for the last two years; dates of any military service; dates of any prior marriages; and claim number of any check you receive from other sources for disability.

A team of trained people in the Disability Determination Services Office will investigate your claim. This office may ask you to take a special physical examination or test. Social Security pays for this and other medical expenses; you will receive a written notification of the decision. If the office approves your claim, the checks generally start with the sixth full month of disability. If the sixth month has passed the first payment could include some back ones.

To determine the amount of your disability payment, Social Security averages your earnings during the previous working years exactly as if you applied for retirement. Benefits usually continue unless your condition has medically improved, and you can perform substantial gainful work. Social Security will periodically review your claim to verify this. This means that the government needs new medical evidence from time to time, or may ask you to undergo a special examination or test. Social Security will pay for these special examinations.

Disability and Your Family

Family members who may also receive payment based on your disability include

1. Your unmarried son or daughter (including stepchild, adopted child, and, in some cases a grandchild) who is under eighteen or under nineteen if in high school full time.
2. Your unmarried son or daughter disabled before twenty-two—benefits may start as early as age eighteen.
3. Your spouse who cares for your child under sixteen or disabled and receiving checks, or who has reached the age of sixty-two or older.
4. Disabled widow or widower, age fifty. The disability must have started before your death or within seven years after death. (If you receive Social Security checks as a widow or widower with children, however, you are eligible if you become disabled before those payments end or within seven years after they end).
5. Disabled surviving divorced spouse if the marriage lasted ten years or longer. Benefits payable at fifty on the same basis as to a disabled widow or widower.

The law recognizes a child's dependency on either parent. This recognition becomes an important factor in disability insurance for women. Suppose as a homemaker under age sixty-two you sell enough of your writing to pay the Social Security tax. If you become disabled, you and your minor or disabled child can draw disability payments.

Returning to Work

The Social Security law has several provisions that may help if you wish to return to work even though you remain disabled.

Vocational rehabilitation services—whether or not your disability claim receives approval—may come from the state vocational rehabilitation agency. Services could include counseling and guidance, medical or surgical help, and job training and placement.

Acceptance of vocational rehabilitation services will not prevent you from securing disability benefits if your claim receives approval. If Social Security offers services, and you refuse them without good reason, Social Security may suspend your monthly benefits.

You can continue receiving full disability benefits for up to nine months while testing your ability to work. You need not work these months consecutively. Generally, only months in which you earn over $75 or spend over fifteen hours in self-employment count as trial work months. After the trial work period, Social Security decides whether or not you can perform any substantial gainful work. If you can, your benefits continue for an additional three-month adjustment period and then stop. If you cannot work at the substantial gainful activity level, disability benefits will continue.

Your earnings provide the biggest factor in determining whether the work activity classifies as substantial gainful employment. If you average over $300 per month gross wages ($700 in 1988 if blind), generally, you are considered to be doing substantial gainful work. However, Social Security considers other factors such as your job duties, hours worked, and any impairment-related medical devices, such as a wheelchair. These expenses may also apply to needs for daily living. The Social Security Administration will determine the deductible and the amount of the deduction in individual cases.

You have special protection for thirty-six months after completing a nine-month trial work period. During this "extended period of eligibility," benefits continue for each and every month you do not perform any substantial gainful activity. You notify Social Security about these months, but you need not file an application to receive benefits for them.

If you receive benefits as a disabled worker and become disabled a second time within five years after benefits stopped (for any reason), the checks can start again with the first full month of the new disability. Social Security does not require another five-month waiting period. This provision also applies if you become entitled to benefits as a person disabled before twenty-two and again within seven years after benefits end.

When you have received disability benefits for twenty-four months, you qualify for medical hospital insurance protection. This benefit pays for hospital care and some follow-up procedures. These months need not come one after the other or in the same disability period. You may also obtain medical insurance Part B. When disability stops, Medicare coverage can continue for two years.

Certain provisions apply to the blind and those with kidney failure. For more information contact your local Social Security office and ask for the free booklet, "Disability."

Medicare

Medicare refers to a federal health insurance program for those sixty-five or older and some previously mentioned disabled people as well as for insured people or their dependents who suffer permanent kidney failure. You apply for Medicare at sixty-five. Medicare consists of two parts: hospital insurance and medical insurance.

Hospital Insurance

Hospital insurance can help pay for medically necessary in-patient hospital care 365 days a year. You pay only a deductible of $564 in 1989 for the first hospital stay each year.

If you need in-patient skilled nursing or rehabilitation services, your insurance pays for up to 150 days in a participating skilled nursing facility each year. Beginning in 1989 Medicare pays all costs except for coinsurance for the first eight days. This equals 20 percent of the average daily cost of skilled nursing care.

When illness confines you to your home after a hospital stay, your insurance pays for the full approved cost of unlimited home health visits from a participating health agency. These services include nursing, physical or speech therapy, part-time home health aides, occupational therapy, medical social services, medical supplies, and equipment.

Under certain conditions hospital insurance can help with the cost of hospice care by a Medicare-certified hospice. In special benefit periods hospice insurance pays for a maximum of two ninety-day periods and one thirty-day period. Medicare, however, will extend hospice coverage as long as necessary when the doctor certifies patient need. Covered services include those of a doctor, nurse, pain killers, and other supplies in addition to those offered under home care. Under hospital care your insurance pays part of the cost for out-patient drugs.

So hospital insurance covers four kinds of care: in-patient hospital, skilled nursing facility after hospital stay, home health care, and hospice care.

You may go to a non-participating United States hospital for an emergency or to the nearest location of the hospital that can handle your need.

You paid for these services when you paid your Social Security tax. You become eligible for these benefits when you retire or at sixty-five if you choose to continue working, and after two years if you become disabled. Under certain conditions your spouse, divorced spouse, widow or widower, dependent parent may become eligible at sixty-five. Disabled widows, widowers, or divorced spouses under sixty-five may qualify along with disabled children eighteen or older. Those with kidney failure qualify at any time.

You get hospital insurance only if you make application for it if you qualify before sixty-five. At sixty-five when you apply for retirement you receive the insurance automatically.

Medical Insurance

Medical insurance, Part B of Medicare, costs you $24.80 per month. You must apply for this insurance.

Medical insurance covers doctors' services, outpatient hospital care, physical therapy, speech pathology services, home health care, and other health costs. This payment begins after you have incurred an annual deductible of $75 in approved charges during the year. Medicare then pays 80 percent of the remaining approved charges for the year.

The Health Care Financing Administration—not Medicare—administers this program. But the people at the Social Security office will help you apply for Medicare and answer your questions about the program. For further details on hospital and medical insurance ask the local Social Security office for the booklet, "Your Medicare Handbook."

Survivors' Insurance

Survivors' insurance covers the dependents of the self-employed writer. Monthly payments for survivors' insurance depend on the same work credits as those for disability. Survivors' insurance goes to the following:

1. Widow or widower. Full benefits at age sixty-five, or any age if caring for an entitled child (under sixteen or disabled) of the deceased worker. Reduced benefits at sixty (or fifty and disabled) if not caring for a child. Remarriage after sixty (fifty if disabled) will not stop benefits provided the worker died before the remarriage by the survivor.
2. Dependent unmarried children under eighteen (nineteen if in high school) or a child disabled before twenty-two.
3. Divorced widow or widower after ten years of marriage. Full benefits at sixty-five, reduced benefits at sixty (fifty if disabled) or any age if caring for an entitled child of the deceased worker. Remarriage after sixty (fifty if disabled) will not stop payments.
4. Divorced widow or widower married less than ten years at any age if caring for an entitled child of the deceased worker.

In addition, grandchildren, great-grandchildren, and dependent parents sixty-two or older may qualify for survivors benefits on the deceased worker's record under certain circumstances.

Social Security computes the benefit payments based on the percentage allotted to the child, widow, widower, or surviving divorced spouse. The pension restriction and Internal Revenue tax placed on other Social Security benefits apply to survivors' payments.

When you apply for these benefits, take your Social Security card or number, the birth certificate of the deceased, the death certificate, the marriage certificate, the divorce papers, birth certificates of children involved, W-2 forms, SE tax returns for the past two years, and any other documents required to support your claim. If you do not have the necessary documents to support your claim, Social Security will help you get them.

Appeals

You have a right to appeal a decision made on any claim. Get the booklet "Your Right to Question the Decision Made on Your Social Security Claim" from your local office. Generally, all procedures follow this routine. First, you ask for a reconsideration and submit any new evidence not previously studied. If you still disagree with the decision, you may request a hearing before an administrative law judge of the Office of Hearings and Appeals. You will find the address in the telephone directory under U.S. Government, Health and Human Services. Your hearing will take place in the location nearest you.

If this outcome proves unsatisfactory, you may request a review by the Appeals Council; Social Security will notify you of the date and place. Finally, you may take your case to a federal court. In each of these steps, you must file within sixty days after you receive the notice of the decision.

You may choose a person to represent you. The leaflet "Social Security and Your Right to Representation" discusses how to select your representative, the duties, and the fees permitted.

Supplementary Security Income

Supplemental Security Income (SSI) pays monthly checks to the aged, disabled, and blind with little income. Social Security runs the program, but money comes from income taxes, not Social Security taxes. The following may qualify for SSI:

1. Person 65 or older.
2. A person under eighteen or older if physically or mentally disabled and cannot work for twelve months or will die.
3. Disabled child under eighteen if the disability grows so severe it keeps the adult from working and will last twelve months or result in death.

4. A blind adult or a child.

The state agency determines disability and blindness cases. It looks at medical conditions (SSA) and at finances. SSI depends on your resources and income.

Resources refer to things you own as real estate, personal belongings, a car, savings and checking accounts, cash, stocks, or bonds. A single adult or child may receive SSI checks with resources up to $1,900 a year or a couple up to $2,850. In determining resources, the agency may consider those of a spouse or parents if child applies, or the sponsor of an alien.

Exclusions as resources include the following: land and home you live in, personal household goods, insurance policy, car if worth less than $4,500 and needed for essential transportation like working or going to the doctor, burial plots, burial funds up to $1,500, or those necessary to earn extra income if disabled or blind.

Income means earnings, such as Social Security checks, pensions, or non-cash items such as food, clothing, and shelter. In determining the amount, Social Security considers the income from a working spouse, parents of a disabled or blind child.

Social Security does exclude the following incomes:

1. First $20 a month of any income.
2. First $65 a month you earn from working. If you earn more than $65, half of the amount does not count. A single person can earn as much as $793 or a couple $1,149.
3. Food stamps.
4. Home energy assistance from certain home energy suppliers.
5. Food, clothing, and shelter from private nonprofit organizations.
6. Necessary equipment for the disabled or expenses a blind person pays to get to work.

Some restrictions automatically make you ineligible. Anyone getting SSI must prove United State citizenship or have immigration papers showing lawful admittance from a foreign country. All must reside in the United States. If you qualify for Social Security or other money benefits, you must apply for them before you apply for SSI, but you can receive both. The disabled must accept vocational rehabilitation services if offered.

Applying for SSI

You apply for the SSI at any Social Security office. Along with your Social Security card and birth certificate, take along any information that establishes your resources and income. If you apply because of blindness or disability, take along medical information such as the names and addresses of doctors and hospitals that have treated you. If you don't have all the information you need, the Social Security office will help you get the necessary papers.

SSI pays $354 a month to an eligible person and $532 to a couple. Generally if you qualify for SSI, you may also get Medicaid to help pay your health care bill. You secure information about Medicaid at your local medical assistance office.

If you find work, you may still draw some money from SSI. As you earn more money, your SSI checks decrease, but you may continue to qualify for Medicaid coverage.

None of these benefits come to you unless you make application for them at the appropriate time. Delaying could cost you money. Your local Social Security office can provide any information or leaflets that pertain to your rights as a self-employed writer. A telephone call may provide the information you need or secure a booklet with the simplified facts. If you don't get the needed information, make an appointment and save much unnecessary waiting at the Social Security office.

Remember, the government does not give you these benefits—you pay for them during your productive years.

Review/Chapter 14

Self-employed writers qualify for Social Security benefits if:
✔they sell their work for a profit
✔they earned a net income of $400 or more a year
✔they write consistently over a period of time
The IRS computes the amount of benefits you qualify for on your earnings once you qualify for fully insured status.

You become fully insured for life when you earn credit for ten years or forty quarters.

Every three years file form SSA7004 to receive a statement.
The other benefits available to you and your family include:
✔disability
✔blindness
✔survivors' insurance
✔Medicare and medical insurance
✔SSI

Chapter 15
The Author's Estate

Arthur F. Abelman

*Planning for the disposition of your assets after your death is diffi-
cult for most people to face. For an author the emotional difficulties
are compounded by literary and artistic considerations. This chapter guides you through the process showing you:*

*1. How and why you must name an executor and why the term
"literary executor" is a misnomer.*

2. How to name a literary advisor for your estate.

3. What the executor does and for how long.

4. What happens to unpublished works.

5. Tax liabilities of author's estates.

*6. How to obtain permission to use works held under authors'
estates.*

The author planning his or her estate is faced with the same problems as any other person, but with some additional difficulties concerning the disposition of literary assets. These assets may include
copyrights, contracts with publishers and other users, and manuscripts, whether completed or not.

Naming an Executor

The first decision the author will face is who is to act as executor
of the author's estate. If the author did not make out a will, an administrator will be appointed by the court to act on all matters concerning the author's estate. The administrator is usually a family
member. The only standards that this person will be required to observe are those imposed by the law of the state in which the author
resides. It is not likely that such an administrator will be familiar
with literary practices or law.

Lawyers are frequently asked whether the author may appoint a
literary executor by will as distinct from an executor to deal with his
other assets. In the United States that is not possible. Consequently,
the author must designate one executor, or several executors, but

they must all have equal responsibility for the author's assets. The customary choice of the executor is between a close relative, an attorney, a bank which handles estate administration, or a trusted friend who has business experience. Sometimes, an individual and a bank are chosen, but this may double the executor's commissions because each may receive a full commission determined by the law of the author's state of residence.

An Adviser Can Be Named

In the case of an author, the executor's duties would include the handling of literary properties and contracts. This is not a commonplace experience for most executors. If the author feels that there is sufficient literary property income to merit the use of a paid adviser, then the author can request or direct that the executor use the services of a named editor or agent to advise with respect to literary matters. A friend with such qualifications might agree to serve at a low fee or no fee but that should be determined before drawing a will. (There is no "average" fee paid to a literary adviser. It might range from zero to several hundred dollars on a very small estate, to a considerable sum on a bestselling author's with many sources of income.) Direction concerning a literary adviser may not be binding on the executor in some states.

The practical method of assuring that the executor will comply with the author's wishes and seek the advice of an experienced adviser is to stipulate that if the executor does rely on such advice, he or she shall not be liable for any mistakes in judgment made by the adviser. In such instances executors would be foolish to rely upon their own judgment when they can avoid liability merely by relying on the adviser, who the author believes is familiar with such matters.

The Executor's Responsibilities

Responsibilites of an executor include making all decisions with respect to the estate that are not mandated by law. This means in simplified terms that the executor must collect all the assets, pay the expenses and the taxes, and then distribute the remaining assets to the beneficiaries under the will. Much paperwork, such as tax return preparation, is required. Banks have specialists who do some of this work, as do some attorneys. The services of an accountant are sometimes required.

When an executor has literary properties to collect and distribute, he or she must notify the publishers and any other contracted users that royalties are to be paid to the estate during the period that the estate is in probate, and then to the named beneficiaries on the closing of the estate. Royalty checks received by an executor payable to a deceased author may be endorsed by the executor and deposited to the estate bank account. The executor also should file a copy of the will in the Copyright Office if the will disposes of copyrights. Later the executor must file in the Copyright Office an assignment from the executor to the beneficiaries under the will. Such papers should name the particular copyrights with as much identifying detail as possible, such as title, author's name, number and date of issuance, as well as the names and interests of the new owners and their percent of ownership when there is more than one; and whether or not a surviving co-owner would take the interest of the deceased co-owner.

Renewing Copyrights

In certain instances the executor of an author's estate may have the responsibility to renew copyrights. Although the Copyright Act of 1976 provides for a system of copyright without renewals for new copyrights, those copyrights that were in their first term on January 1, 1978, the effective date of the present Copyright Act, must be renewed. The statute gives the right to renew such copyrights (unless the work is a work made for hire as defined in the Copyright Act) to the individual author if that author is still living, or the widow or widower or children of the author if the author is not living. But if the author, widow or widower, or children are not living, then the right to renew goes to the author's executors. A renewal made in the name of an improper party does not constitute a valid renewal so that the executor must review these provisions of the Copyright Act very carefully to determine who may renew. Once an executor is discharged of duties and the estate is closed, he or she will not have power to renew copyrights which may come up for renewal. Such renewals must be made by the next of kin.

The Copyright Act grants a right of termination of transfers and licenses of any right under a copyright to authors and certain of their survivors. Rights of termination of transfers and licenses (including publishing contracts) under the Copyright Act are a subject beset with technicalities that even skilled attorneys have misunderstood. In general, the termination right passes on the author's death to the author's widow or widower, children, and to grandchildren after their parents' death, but not to executors. If no one named in the Copyright Act survives, no one may exercise the right to termination of transfers and licenses.

What About Unpublished Works?

An author can direct that the executor shall seek publication of all unpublished works, or that the executor shall not publish certain of the author's unpublished works. He or she may also restrict certain types of publication and any other use by will. The will may also provide that a period of time must elapse before publication. The executor will not be responsible to the beneficiaries of the estate should such executor, after exercising due care and diligence, be unable to find a publisher. An executor would probably be unable to arrange for a vanity or subsidized publication without specific authorization in the will, because it would convey no benefit to the estate.

The author should indicate in a will who the recipients of copyrights, contracts, and royalties will be. If the author fails to do so, they will pass under what is called a "residuary clause" if there is one in the will. A residuary clause purports to dispose of the "rest, residue, and remainder of my property." If there is no residuary clause and no direct bequest of the author's copyrights, contracts, and royalties, then there is a so-called partial intestacy under the will, and the copyrights, contracts, and royalties will pass under the state intestacy laws—usually to the next of kin.

Although the author may dispose by will of copyrights, contracts, and royalties, an author may not dispose by will of renewal copyrights that arise after his or her death. The reason is that Congress has created the renewal copyright property and has given it to the author only if alive. If the author is not alive at the time of renewal, he or she does not own the renewal copyright and it passes under the Copyright Act as provided in that act.

Trust Funds

Authors may wish to set up living or testamentary trust funds for children or other beneficiaries to receive royalties. It is done in the same way as any other trust fund except that the copyrights and contracts become the so-called "corpus" of the trust fund, which means the property held in trust, and the royalties will then be paid to the designated children. The author might require that a portion of the royalties be retained or paid at a later date, but that must be specified in the will or the executors will be required to pay out the royalties to the designated beneficiaries of the trust. The language of a trust should be drafted by a lawyer because all such matters are governed by a large and technical body of law which varies from state to state. Similar considerations exist in selecting a trustee as in the selection of an executor.

An author may require that the executor keep records of income with respect to literary and other properties. It is not customary to provide this because by law, in most states, executors are required to do so. Furthermore, for their own protection they will do so in order to show that they have properly executed their fiduciary responsibilities under the estate. This would include keeping a record of all copyright certificates, contracts, and all royalties or fees received and to whom paid. This in not very different from the executor's responsibility in keeping records of all other assets in the estate including stocks, bonds, and other financial investments and the disposition of income from such investments. The final records will include an assignment of copyrights and contracts to the beneficiaries followed by some form of accounting by the executor to the probate court.

State Tax Policies Vary

The tax situation of authors is not different from the point of view of estate tax from all other persons. The federal net estate will have to be $600,000 or greater before it is taxed. Net estate means the assets less the debts of the deceased and the expenses of the estate. This includes accounting fees, executor's commissions, lawyer's fees, etc. On a state level the picture is much more varied. Some states do not tax the estates of their deceased citizens. Others impose small inheritance or estate taxes; some states impose large taxes. New York, which is a high-taxing jurisdiction, does not tax an estate until it reaches $108,000 of net assets.

Executors' commissions vary from state to state. Some states allow the probate judge to fix a reasonable compensation. In other states the executor's commission is fixed by statue as a percentage of the estate, but the percentage varies.

If an author wishes to make a gift to his or her spouse, there is usually no tax on such gift by will. The same would not be true of gifts to children, parents, brothers and sisters, or close friends. Charitable gifts are usually tax exempt.

Using Works that Belong to an Estate

If an author wishes to use works belonging to an estate either alone or in conjunction with his or her work, he or she may obtain that permission in two ways. First, if the author knows the names and addresses of the executor of an estate of a deceased author, you may apply directly for permission. That is not always the easiest information to determine quickly. The customary practice is to write to the publisher of the work you propose to use, state the use you wish to make of it and the terms that you are offering.

For example, if you wish to use two stanzas of a poem in a third-grade English reader that will be published in the United States only, you should include all such information in the permission request. You might also include information concerning the fee you are willing to pay. In most instances, the amount of the fee is requested by the proposed user without making an offer in the first letter, but this prolongs the process of obtaining permission because further correspondence will be required to answer the fee inquiry and to confirm that it is acceptable.

Sometimes the publisher will secure permissions for the author, but most contracts between author and publisher place this burden on the author. When the publisher of a work for which permission is sought receives such a letter, the publisher either has obtained authority from the estate of its author to grant such permission or will forward the request to the executor or agent for action by the estate. There is no requirement that an estate grant permission to an author to reproduce its work any more than there is such requirement that a living author grant such permission.

However, executors are under an obligation to entertain fairly all such offers and to make grants to proper parties when the grant will be remunerative for the beneficiaries of the estate (unless expressly prohibited by the terms of the will). This means there is a slightly better chance of obtaining a permission from an estate than from a living author because a living author may refuse permission even though such refusal would be to his or her economic disadvantage. In other words, executors may not act by whim or against the financial interests of the estate. If you cannot locate an author, his or her executor, or estate, you do not have a right to use without permission and must delete such material or take the risk that such use will infringe.

If an author wishes to stop his or her executor from granting permissions, it should be provided in the will. This might be done if an author does not favor use of his or her work on merchandise or in connection with a particular form of publication. If the author is simply interested in the money that will be returned to the estate from contracts for use of literary work, there is no reason to restrict, and the author should request the executor to affirmatively seek such contracts (even though the executor is under a duty to give fair consideration to all responsible offers to use the author's work).

Finally, an author will be well advised, as would most other people, to consult with his or her lawyer about an estate plan. State laws vary and the author should obtain the benefit of counsel on such laws. The amount of taxes payable as estate taxes will also vary from state to state. This article is not meant to be exhaustive or to be used to prepare a will. It's meant to help authors understand estate problems so they can question an attorney and arrive at a plan that will be satisfactory.

Review/Chapter 15

Part of an author's estate are literary properties that include:
  ✔copyrights, assigned and unassigned
  ✔contracts
  ✔manuscripts, finished and unfinished
There are two basic ways to handle literary estates:
  ✔naming as executor somone with experience in literary property.
  ✔naming a paid literary advisor to the estate.
Unpublished works can be handled in several ways:

✔the author can direct the executor to seek publication with restrictions and limitations if desired

✔or direct that publication not be sought or be sought after a certain period of time has elasped.

The power to renew copyrights:

✔passes by statute to the widow/widower and children

✔or if the widow/widower and children are deceased the executor
may renew.

About the Authors

Arthur F. Abelman is an attorney in New York who is of counsel to the firm of Moses & Singer. He has specialized for more than twenty years in law relating to publishing, entertainment, and the arts. He is a graduate of Harvard College and Harvard Law School.

Louise Boggess is a Phi Beta Kappa from the University of Texas, whose M.A. included a major in government. She married a fellow student who majored in law. Her book, *Your Social Security Benefits* (Funk and Wagnalls), provided the background for her chapter on Social Security in this book. Her other books include *Journey to Citizenship* (Funk and Wagnalls), about the immigration laws, and three in the writing field: *Article Techniques That Sell, How to Write Short Stories That Sell* (Writer's Digest Books), and *How to Write Fillers and Short Features That Sell* (Harper & Row). She coauthored with her husband, Bill Boggess, *American Brilliant Cut Glass* (Crown, Inc.) and *Identifying American Brilliant Cut Glass* (Crown, Inc.).

Georges Borchardt is the president and founder of Georges Borchardt, Inc., a New York literary agency. He recently taught a course in literary agenting at City University of New York, has written articles on contracts and royalty statements for *Publishers Weekly*, and has lectured on publishing at Columbia, Harvard, Johns Hopkins, University of California—Los Angeles, University of Southern California, and Washington University. He has served on the board of the Society of Authors' Representatives and recently completed a two-year term as treasurer of PEN—American Center.

Herald Price Fahringer is a practicing lawyer in New York City who has defended obscenity prosecutions throughout the United States. He defended *Hustler Magazine* in Cincinnati and Al Goldstein, the publisher of *Screw*, in Wichita, Kansas. He is general counsel to the First Amendment Lawyers Association.

Patricia Fox Fleck has been a copywriter and continuity director for radio stations in New Jersey and Pennsylvania. She's published articles in America, Canada, and Great Britain and has won awards for her fiction at writers' conferences and in the *Writer's Digest* Creative Writing Contest.

William E. Francois is a professor emeritus of journalism at Drake University, Des Moines, Iowa, where he taught communication law for fifteen years. He is the author of four books, including *Mass Media Law & Regulation*, which is widely used as a college textbook. He also has written several hundred magazine articles and for three years wrote a monthly column for *Writer's Digest* entitled "Law & the Writer," which won two American Bar Association certificates of merit

for outstanding service in connection with making the law more un-
derstandable. Francois, a college journalism teacher for twenty-nine
years, also was a newspaper reporter/editor for ten years.

Laury M. Frieber is a graduate of the University of California at
Berkeley and Hastings College of the Law. After four years in private
practice in New York City, she joined Time Inc. in 1986 and is presently Associate Counsel in the company's Magazine Group.

Harry M. Johnston III is a graduate of Columbia College of Columbia University and the New York University Law School. From 1968 to
1970 he served as a VISTA volunteer attorney and then joined Time
Inc. He is Vice President and General Counsel of the Time Inc. Magazine Group.

Perry Knowlton has been president of the New York literary
agency, Curtis Brown, Ltd., since 1968. Prior to that, he served as
vice president and head of the book division for that agency, coming
to the position from Charles Scribner's Sons, where he was an editor
in the trade division. Knowlton has twice been vice president and
head of the literary branch of the Society of Authors' Representatives
and has also served a six-year term as president.

Michael S. Lasky has written for dozens of top national
magazines, including *Parade, Playboy, Esquire, Gentleman's Quarterly, Family Health, Writer's Digest* and the *New York Times.* He is
author of *The Complete Junk Food Book* (McGraw-Hill) and *The
Films of Alfred Hitchcock* (Citadel Press). Currently an editor for a
national computer magazine, he was formerly associate editor of *Fo-
lio: The Magazine for Magazine Management* for which his article
on libel was originally prepared.

Richard H. Logan III was professor of journalism at Mississippi
University for Women and had taught photography and journalism in
colleges and universities in Florida, Texas, and Mississippi for some
twenty-one years before retiring in 1979. He formerly worked as a
photographer and reporter for daily newspapers and operated his
own advertising and industrial photography agency. He received his
Ph.D. degree from the University of Southern Mississippi and has
received professional honors for his work both as an educator and as
a photographer.

Victor W. Marton has worked for the Copyright Office, Libary of
Congress for more than twelve years and is currently head of the Information Section. He is a member of the American Bar Association
and the bar of the Commonwealth of Pennsylvania. He received a Juris Doctor degree from the Columbus School of Law of the Catholic
University of America in 1987, an M.P.A. from George Washington
University in 1975, and a B.A. degree from St. Vincent College in
1972.

Richard S. Newcombe founded Creators Syndicate in 1987, after
two years as president and chief executive officer of News America

Syndicate. Prior to that he served as vice president and general manager of the Los Angeles Times Syndicate for six years. He is on the board of directors of the Newspaper Features Council.

Carol Rinzler is an attorney with Rembar & Curtis, a New York law firm that represents publishers and authors. She is a contributing editor of *Publishers Weekly*, for which she writes articles on legal issues of interest to publishers.

Lionel S. Sobel is a professor at Loyola Law School in Los Angeles where he teaches copyright and entertainment law. He is also the editor of the *Entertainment Law Reporter*, a monthly periodical read by entertainment lawyers and industry executives. Sobel is a graduate of the UCLA School of Law (1969) and the University of California, Berkeley (1966). Before joining the faculty at Loyola, he was in private practice in Beverly Hills.

Theodore Stellwag is executive director of the Pennsylvania Bar Association. His "Reporter's Guide to Legalese," from which the glossary in this book was excerpted, was created for those persons assigned to cover courts in Pennsylvania and for editors and station managers. He is a former newspaper columnist and court reporter for newspapers in New Jersey and Pennsylvania.

A Glossary of Legal Terms

(Condensed from *The Reporter's Guide to Legalese and the Courts*, courtesy Theodore Stellwag, Pennsylvania Bar Association.)

A

abstract of title—A chronological history, in abbreviated form, of the ownership of a parcel of land.

action in personam—An action against the person, founded on a personal liability.

action in rem—An action for the recovery of a specific object, usually an item of personal property such as an automobile.

adjudication—Giving or pronouncing a judgment or decree; also the judgment given.

adversary system—The system of trial practice in which each of the opposing, or adversary, parties has full opportunity to present and establish opposing contentions before the court.

allegation—The declaration made in a pleading, setting out what one expects to prove.

amicus curiae—A friend of the court; one who interposes, with the permission of the court, to volunteer information upon some matter of law.

answer—A pleading by which the defendant endeavors to resist the plaintiff's allegation of facts.

appearance—The formal proceeding by which a party submits himself to the jurisdiction of the court.

appellant—The party appealing a decision or judgment—which he considers incorrect—to a higher court.

appellate court—A court having jurisdiction of appeal and review; not a "trial court."

appellee—The party against whom an appeal is taken.

arraignment—In criminal practice, to bring a prisoner to court to answer to a criminal charge.

at issue—A case is said to be "at issue" when the pleadings have been completed and the case is ready for trial before either a judge or a jury.

attachment—The act of taking, apprehending, or seizing persons or property by writ, summons, or order to bring the person or property into legal custody. Used to bring a person to court, acquire jurisdiction over seized property, compel appearances, furnish securities for a debt or costs, and to seize a fund in the hands of a third person.

B

bail—Security given for the release of an arrested person to assure his appearance in court.

bail bond—An obligation signed by the accused, with sureties, to secure his presence in court.

bailiff—A court attendant whose duties are to keep order in the courtroom and to have custody of the jury.

bench warrant—A warrant issued from the court for the attachment or arrest of a person.

best evidence—Primary evidence, as distinguished from secondary; the best and highest evidence of which the nature of the case is susceptible.

brief—A written or printed document prepared by the counsel to file in court, usually setting forth both facts and law in support of his case.

burden of proof—In the law of evidence, the necessity or duty of affirmatively proving a fact or facts in dispute.

C

case law—See common law.

change of venue—The removal of a suit begun in one county or district to another, for trial, or from one court to another in the same county or district.

circumstantial evidence—All evidence of indirect nature; the process of decision by which court or jury may reason from circumstances known or proved to establish by inference the principal fact.

code—A collection, compendium, or revision of laws systematically arranged into chapters, table of contents, and index and promulgated by legislative authority.

codicil—A supplement or an addition to a will.

common law—Law that derives its authority solely from usages and customs of immemorial antiquity, or from the judgments and decrees of courts. Also called "case law."

commutation—The change of a punishment from a greater degree to a lesser degree, as from death to life imprisonment.

comparative negligence—The degrees of "slight," "ordinary," and "gross" negligence, often expressed in percentages and used to compare acts of opposing parties.

complainant—Synonymous with "plaintiff."

condemnation—The legal process by which real estate of a private owner is taken for public use without his consent, but upon the award and payment of just compensation.

contempt of court—Any action calculated to embarrass, hinder, or obstruct a court in the administration of justice, or calculated to lessen its authority or dignity. Contempts are of two kinds: direct and indirect. Direct contempts are those committed in the immediate presence of the court; indirect is the term chiefly used with reference to the failure or refusal to obey a lawful order.

contract—An oral or written agreement between two or more parties that is enforceable by law.

corpus delicti—The body (material substance) upon which a crime has been committed, e.g., the corpse of a murdered man, the charred remains of a burned house.

costs—An allowance for expenses in prosecuting or defending a suit. Ordinarily this does not include attorney's fees.

counterclaim—A claim presented by a defendant in opposition to the claim of a plaintiff.

courts of record—Those whose proceedings are permanently recorded, and have the power to find or imprison for contempt. Courts not of record are those of lesser authority whose proceedings are not permanently recorded.

D

damages—Pecuniary compensation that may be recovered in the courts by any person who has suffered loss, detriment, or injury to his person, property, or rights, through the unlawful act or negligence of another.

declaratory judgment—One that declares the rights of the parties or expresses the opinion of the court on a question of law, without ordering anything to be done.

decree—A decision or order of the court. A final decree is one that fully and finally disposes of the litigation; an interlocutory is a provisional or preliminary decree that is not final.

defamation—The use of false, derogatory statements about another. Verbal statements constitute "slander." Written statements constitute "libel."

default—A "default" in an action at law occurs when a party omits to plead within the time allowed or fails to appear at the trial.

demur—To file a pleading (called "a demurrer"), admitting the truth of the facts in the complaint, or answer, but contending they are legally insufficient.

deposition—The testimony of a witness not taken in open court, but in pursuance of a rule of court.

direct evidence—Proof of facts by witnesses who saw acts done or heard words spoken as distinguished from circumstantial evidence, which is called indirect.

direct examination—The first interrogation of a witness by the attorney for the party on whose behalf he is called.

directed verdict—An instruction by the judge to the jury to return a specified verdict.

discovery—A proceeding whereby one party to an action may be informed as to facts known by other parties or witnesses.

domicile—That place where a person has his true and permanent home. A person may have several residences, but only one domicile.

double jeopardy—Common-law and constitutional prohibition against more than one prosecution for the same crime.

due process—Law in its regular course through the courts. The guarantee of due process assures every person a fair trial in both civil and criminal actions, after notice is given and the person has an opportunity to be heard.

E

embezzlement—The fraudulent appropriation by a person to his own use or benefit of property or money entrusted to him by another.

eminent domain—The power to take private property for public use by condemnation.

enjoin—To require a person, by writ of injunction from a court of equity, to perform or to abstain or desist from some act.

entrapment—The act of officers or agents of a government in inducing a person to commit a crime not contemplated by him, for the purpose of instituting a criminal prosecution against him.

escheat—In American law, the right of the state to property to which no one is able to make a valid claim.

escrow—An arrangement whereby a deed or other writing, money, or securities are placed in the hands of a third person to be held until the occurrence of a specified contingency, performance of a specified condition, or receipt of a specified notice authorizing release.

estoppel—A person's own act, or acceptance of facts, which precludes his later making claims to the contrary.

ex parte—By or for one party; done for, in behalf of or on the application of one party only.

ex post facto—After the fact; an act or fact occurring after some previous act or fact, and relating thereto.

executor—A person named by the decedent in his will to carry out the provisions of that will.

extradition—The surrender by one state to another of an individual accused or convicted of an offense outside its own territory, and within the territorial jurisdiction of the other.

F

fair comment—A term used in the law of libel, applying to statements made by a writer in an honest belief of their truth, even though the statements are not true in fact.

felony—A crime of a graver nature than a misdemeanor. Generally, an offense punishable by death or imprisonment in a penitentiary.

fiduciary—A term derived from the Roman law, meaning a person holding the character of a trustee, with obligations of trust, confidence, scrupulous good faith, and candor.

forgery—The false making or material altering, with intent to defraud, of any writing which, if genuine, might be the foundation of a legal liability.

fraud—An intentional perversion of truth; deceitful practice or device resorted to with intent to deprive another of property or other right, or in some manner to do him injury.

G

garnishment—A proceeding whereby property, money, or credits of a debtor in the possession of another (the garnishee) are applied to the debts of the debtor.

garnishee—The person upon whom a garnishment is served, usually a person holding assets of a debtor.

guardian ad litem—A person appointed by the court to represent the interests or potential interests of a minor, an incompetent or possible, unborn baby, whose interests in property may be affected by the court's decree.

H

habeas corpus—"You have the body." The name given a variety of writs whose object is to bring a person before a court or judge. In most common usage, it is directed to the official or person detaining another, commanding him to produce the body of the prisoner or person detained so the court may determine if such person has been denied his liberty without due process of law.

harmless error—In appellate practice, an error committed by a lower court during a trial, but not prejudicial to the rights of the losing party and for which the court will not reverse the judgment.

hearsay—Evidence not proceeding from the personal knowledge of the witness.

holographic will—A will written in the testator's own handwriting, as opposed to the invalid noncupative will that is declared orally by the testator before a sufficient number of witnesses and afterwards reduced to writing.

hostile witness—A witness who is subject to cross-examination by the party who called him to testify, because of his evident antagonism toward that party as exhibited in his direct examination.

hypothetical question—A combination of facts and circumstances, assumed or proved, stated in such a form as to constitute a coherent state of facts upon which the opinion of an expert can be asked by way of evidence in a trial.

I

impeachment of witness—An attack on the credibility of a witness by the testimony of other witnesses.

implied contract—A contract in which the promise made by the obligor is not expressed, but inferred by his conduct or implied in law.

imputed negligence—Negligence that is not directly attributable to a person, but to another who has a joint legal interest and with whose fault he is chargeable.

inadmissible—That which, under the established rules of evidence, cannot be admitted or received.

incompetent evidence—Evidence that is not admissible because, even if accepted, it would not tend to prove the allegation involved.

indeterminate sentence—An indefinite sentence of "not less than" and "not more than" so many years, the exact term to be served being afterwards determined by parole authorities with the minimum and maximum limits set by the court or by statute.

indictment—An accusation in writing by a grand jury, charging that a person has done some act, or been guilty of some omission, which, by law, is a crime.

inferior court—Any court subordinate to the chief appellate tribunal in a particular judicial system.

information—An accusation for some criminal offense, in the nature of an indictment, from which it differs only in being presented by a competent public officer instead of a grand jury.

injunction—A mandatory or prohibitive writ issued by a court.

instruction—A direction given by the judge to the jury concerning the law of the case.

interlocutory—Provisional; temporary; not final. Refers to orders and decrees of a court.

interrogatories—Formal written questions used in the judicial examination of a party, who must provide written answers under oath.

intervention—A proceeding in a suit or action by which a third person is permitted by the court to make himself a party.

intestate—One who dies without leaving a will.

irrelevant—Evidence not relating or applicable to the matter in issue; not supporting the issue.

J

jurisprudence—The philosophy of law, or the science that deals with the principles of positive law and legal relations.

jury—A certain number of people, selected according to law, and sworn to inquire of certain matters of fact, and declare the truth upon evidence laid before them.

grand jury—A jury whose duty is to receive complaints and accusations in criminal cases, hear the evidence, and find bills of indictment in cases where they are satisfied a trial ought to be had.

petit jury—The jury of 12 (or fewer) persons for the trial of a civil or criminal case.

jury commissioner—An officer charged with the duty of selecting the names to be put into a jury wheel, or of drawing the panel of jurors for a particular term of court.

L

leading question—One that instructs a witness how to answer or puts into his mouth words to be echoed back; one that suggests to the witness the answer desired. Prohibited on direct examination.

levy—The legal process whereby property may be seized and sold to satisfy a judgment or debt.

libel—A method of defamation expressed by print, writing, pictures, or signs. In its most general sense any publication that is untruthfully injurious to the reputation of another.

lis pendens—A pending suit.

locus delicti—The place of the offense.

M

malfeasance—Evil doing; ill conduct; the commission of some act that is positively prohibited by law.

malicious prosecution—An action instituted with intention of injuring a defendant without probable cause, and which terminates in favor of the person prosecuted.

mandamus—The name of a writ that issues from a court of superior jurisdiction, directed to an inferior court, commanding the performance of a particular act.

mandate—A judicial command or precept proceeding from a court or judicial officer, directing the proper officer to enforce a judgment, sentence, or decree.

manslaughter—The unlawful killing of another without malice; may be either voluntary, upon a sudden impulse, or involuntary, in the commission of some unlawful act.

master—An officer of the court, usually an attorney, appointed for the purpose of taking testimony and making a report to the court, most frequently in divorce cases.

material evidence—Such as is relevant and goes to the substantial issues in dispute.

misdemeanor—Offenses less than felonies; generally those punishable by fine or imprisonment other than in penitentiaries.

misfeasance—A misdeed or trespass. The improper performance of some act that a person may lawfully do, such as misconduct by a public official in performance of an official discretionary act, with an improper motive, e.g. for personal gain.

mistrial—A trial terminated by the court because of some error or prejudice developing during the trial.

mitigating circumstance—One that does not constitute a justification or excuse of an offense, but which may be considered as reducing the degree of liability.

moot—Unsettled; undecided. A moot point is one not settled by judicial decision.

moral turpitude—Conduct contrary to honesty, modesty, or good morals.

municipal courts—In the judicial organization of some states, courts whose territorial authority is confined to the city or community.

murder—The unlawful killing of a human being by another with malice aforethought, either express or implied.

N

negligence—The omission to do something that a reasonable man, guided by ordinary consideration, would do; or the doing of something that a reasonable and prudent man would not do.

next friend—One acting for the benefit of an infant or other person without being regularly appointed as guardian.

nolle prosequi—A formal entry into the record by the plaintiff in a civil suit, or the prosecuting officer in a criminal case, in which it is declared that he "will no further prosecute" the case.

nolo contendere—Literally, "I will not contest it." A pleading that denies the guilt but admits the fact on which the charge is based.

nominal party—One who is joined as a party or defendant merely because the technical rules of pleading require his presence in the record.

non obstante veredicto—Notwithstanding the verdict. A judgment entered by order of court for one party, although there has been a jury verdict against him.

notice to produce—A notice in writing requiring the opposite party to produce a certain paper or document at the trial.

O

objection—The act of taking exception to some statement or procedure in trial. Used to call the court's attention to improper evidence or procedure.

of counsel—A phrase commonly applied to counsel employed to assist in the preparation or management of the case, or its presentation on appeal, but who is not the principal attorney of record.

opinion evidence—Evidence of what the witness thinks, believes, or infers in regard to fact in dispute, as distinguished from his personal knowledge of the facts; not admissible except (under certain limitations) in the case of experts.

out of court—One who has no legal status in court is said to be "out of court," i.e., he is not before the court. For example, when a plaintiff, by some act of omission or commission, shows that he is unable to maintain his action, he is frequently said to have put himself "out of court."

P

panel—A list of jurors to serve in a particular court, or for the trial of a particular action; denotes either the whole body of persons summoned as jurors for a particular term of court or those selected by the clerk by lot.

parties—The persons who are actively concerned in the prosecution or defense of any legal proceeding.

peremptory challenge—The challenge that the prosecution or defense may use to reject a certain number of prospective jurors without assigning any cause.

plaintiff—A person who institutes an action; the party who complains or sues in a legal action.

plaintiff in error—The party who obtains a writ of error to have a judgment or other proceeding at law reviewed by an appellate court.

pleading—The process by which the parties in a suit or action alternately present written statements of their contentions, each responsive to that which precedes and each serving to narrow the field of controversy, until there evolves a single disputed point called the "issue" upon which they then go to trial.

polling the jury—A practice whereby the jurors are asked individually whether they assented, and still assent, to the verdict.

power of attorney—An instrument authorizing another to act as one's agent or attorney.

praecipe—An original writ commanding the defendant to do the thing required; also, an order addressed to the clerk of a court, requesting him to issue a particular writ.

prejudicial error—Synonymous with "reversible error"; an error that warrants the appellate court in reversing the judgment before it.

preliminary hearing—Synonymous with "preliminary examination"; the hearing given a person charged with crime by a magistrate or judge to determine whether he should be held for trial.

preponderance of evidence—Greater weight of evidence, or evidence that is more credible and convincing to the mind, not necessarily the greater number of witnesses.

presentment—An informal statement in writing by a grand jury to the court that a crime has been committed, from their own knowledge or observation, without any bill of indictment laid before them.

presumption of facts—An inference as to the truth or falsity of any proposition or fact, drawn by a process of reasoning in the absence of actual certainty of its truth or falsity, or until such certainty can be ascertained.

presumption of law—A rule of law that courts and judges shall draw a particular inference from a particular fact, or from particular evidence.

probate—The process of proving a will.

probation—In modern criminal administration, allowing a convicted person (particularly juvenile offenders) to go at large, under a suspension of sentence, during good behavior, and generally under the supervision or guardianship of a probation officer.

prosecutor—The instigator of prosecution against an arrested person or accusation against a suspect. Also, one who takes charge of a case as a trial lawyer for the people.

Q

quasi judicial—The nature of the authority or discretion of an officer when that officer's acts become judicial.

quid pro quo—"What for what," a fair return or consideration.

quo warranto—A judicial writ requiring an individual to show by what right he undertakes to exercise the authority of a particular office or position.

R

reasonable doubt—The state of the minds of jurors in which they cannot say they feel an abiding conviction as to the truth of the charge. An accused person is entitled to acquittal if, in the minds of the jury, the accused's guilt has not been proved beyond a "reasonable doubt."

rebuttal—The introduction of rebutting evidence; the showing that statements of witnesses as to what occurred are not true; the stage of a trial at which such evidence may be introduced.

redirect examination—Follows cross-examination, and is done by the party who first examined the witness.

referee—An officer to whom a pending cause is referred to take testimony and report back to the court. The referee exercises judicial powers as an arm of the court for that specific purpose.

removal, order of—An order by a court directing the transfer of a case to another court.

reply—When a case is tried or argued in court, the argument of the plaintiff in answer to that of the defendant. A pleading in response to an answer.

rest—A party is said to "rest" or "rest his case" when he has presented all the evidence he intends to offer.

retainer—An act of the client in employing his attorney or counsel; also denotes the fee that the client pays when he retains the attorney to act for him.

robbery—The taking or stealing of property from another with force or the threat of force.

rule nisi, or rule to show cause—A decision or order of a court that will become final unless the party against whom it is directed files an exception or an appeal or otherwise complies with the order.

S

search and seizure, unreasonable—Generally, an examination made of premises or person without legal authority, to discover stolen contraband, illicit property, or some evidence of guilt.

search warrant—An order in writing, issued by a justice or magistrate in the name of the state, directing an officer to search a specified house or other premises for evidence. Usually required as a condition precedent to a legal search and seizure.

self-defense—The protection of one's person or property against some injury attempted by another. The law of "self defense" justifies an act done in the reasonable belief of immediate danger. When acting in justifiable self-defense, a person may not be punished criminally or held responsible for civil damages.

separate maintenance—Allowance granted to a wife for support of herself and children while she is living apart from her husband but not divorced from him.

separation of witnesses—An order of the court requiring all witnesses to remain outside the courtroom until each is called to testify, except the plaintiff and defendant.

sheriff—An officer of a county, usually chosen by popular election, whose principal duties are to aid the criminal and civil court; chief preserver of the peace. He serves processes, summons juries, executes judgments, and holds judicial sales.

sine qua non—An indispensable requisite.

slander—Base and defamatory spoken words tending to prejudice another in his reputation, business, or means of livelihood. "Libel" and "slander" both are methods of defamation, the former being expressed by print, writings, pictures, or signs; the latter orally.

specific performance—Where money damages would be inadequate compensation for the breach of an obligation, the defaulting party will be compelled to perform specifically what he has agreed to do.

stare decisis—The doctrine that, when a court has once laid down a principal of law as applicable to a certain set of facts, it will adhere to that principle and apply it to future cases where the facts are substantially the same.

state's evidence—Testimony given by an accomplice or joint participant in a crime, tending to incriminate others, and given under an actual or implied promise of immunity.

statute—The written law as opposed to the unwritten law.

stay—A stopping or arresting of a judicial proceeding by order of the court.

stipulation—An agreement by opposing attorneys with respect to any matter involved in the proceedings. Stipulations must be either in writing filed with an approval by the court, or read into the record during the proceedings.

subpeona—A process to cause a witness to appear and give testimony before a court or magistrate.

subpeona duces tecum—A process by which the court commands a witness to produce certain documents or records in a trial.

substantive law—The law dealing with rights, duties, and liabilities, as distinguished from adjective law that regulates procedure.

summons—A writ directing the sheriff or other officer to notify the named person that an action has been commenced against him in court and that he is required to appear, on the day named, and answer the complaint in such action.

supersedeas—A writ containing a command to stay proceedings at law, such as the enforcement of a judgment pending an appeal.

T

testimony—Evidence given by a witness, under oath; as distinguished from evidence derived from writing and other sources.

tort—An injury or wrong committed, either with or without force, to the person or property of another.

transcript—The official record of proceedings in a trial or hearing.

trial de novo—A new trial or retrial in an appellate court in which the whole case is gone into as if no trial had been held in a lower court.

true bill—In criminal practice, the endorsement made in a grand jury upon a bill of indictment when they find it sufficient to warrant a criminal charge.

U

undue influence—Whatever destroys free will and causes a person to do something he would not do if left to himself.

unlawful detainer—A detention of real estate without the consent of the owner or other person entitled to its possession.

usury—The taking of more interest for the use of money than the law allows.

V

venire—Technically, a writ summoning persons to court to act as jurors; popularly used as meaning the body of names thus summoned.

veniremen—Members of a panel of jurors.

venue—The particular county, city, or geographical area in which a court with jurisdiction may hear and determine a case.

verdict—The formal decision or finding made by a jury, reported to the court, and accepted by it.

voir dire—To speak the truth. The phrase denotes the preliminary examination that the court or counsel makes of a potential witness or juror, as to his qualifications.

W

waiver of immunity—A means authorized by statutes by which a witness, in advance of giving testimony or producing evidence, may renounce the fundamental right guaranteed by the Constitution that no person shall be compelled to be a witness against himself.

warrant of arrest—A writ issued by a magistrate, justice, or other competent authority to a sheriff or other officer, requiring him to arrest the person therein named and bring him before the magistrate or court to answer to a specified charge.

weight of evidence—The balance or preponderance of evidence; the inclination of the greater amount of credible evidence, offered in a trial, to support one side of the issue rather than the other.

willful—A "willful" act is one done intentionally without justifiable cause, as distinguished from an act done carelessly or inadvertently.

with prejudice—The term, as applied to judgment of dismissal, is a final disposition of a case.

without prejudice—A dismissal "without prejudice" allows a new suit to be brought on the same claim.

witness—One who testifies to what he has seen, heard, or otherwise observed.

writ—An order issuing from a court requiring the performance of a specified act, or giving authority and commission to have it done.

Bibliography

Books & Library Reference Volumes

Advertising Compliance Handbook, 1988, Practising Law Institute, New York
Advertising Law Anthology, Volume XI, 1987, Bethesda, Maryland
American Jurisprudence 2d, Lawyers Co-operative Publishing, Rochester
Ballentine's Law Dictionary with Pronunciations, Lawyers Co-operative Publishing, Rochester
Book Publishing 1988, Practising Law Institute, New York
Business, Media and the Law, New York University Press, New York
Cases and Materials on Copyright and Other Aspects of Entertainment Litigation Illustrated Including Unfair Competition, Defamation, Privacy, third edition, 1985, West Publishing, St. Paul
Communications Law, 1987, Practising Law Institute, New York
Computer Software: Protection, Liability, Law, Forms, Clark Boardman, New York
Copyright Law: A Practitioner's Guide, Practising Law Institute, New York
The Copyright Primer for Librarians and Educators, American Library Association, Chicago, Illinois
Corpus Juris Secundum, West Publishing Co., St. Paul
Current Developments in Copyright Law 1988, Practising Law Institute, New York
Dictionary of Legal Abbreviations Used in American Law Books, second edition, William S. Hein and Company, Buffalo
Directory of Intellectual Property Lawyers and Patent Agents 1988–89 edition, Clark Boardman Co., Ltd., New York
Entertainment, Publishing and the Arts Handbook, 1988, Clark Boardman Co., Ltd., New York
Film/TV Law, 1973, Seven Arts Press, Hollywood
Free But Regulated; Conflicting Traditions in Media Law, Iowa State University Press, Ames, Iowa
How to Register a Copyright and Protect Your Creative Work, 1987, Charles Scribner's Sons, New York
In Tune with the Music Business, Law Arts Publishers, New York
An Intellectual Property Law Primer, Clark Boardman Co., Ltd., New York
The Journalist's Handbook on Libel and Privacy, Free Press, New York
Law Books in Print, 5th edition, 1987, Glanville Publishers, Inc., Dobbs Ferry, New York
Law and Legal Information Directory, 1988, Gale Research Company, Detroit
Law and the Television of the 80's, 1983, Oceana Publications, Inc., New York
Law Dictionary, Barrons' Educational Series, Inc., Hauppauge, New York
Law of Advertising, The, Matthew Bender & Company, New York

LDRC 50-State Survey 1987, Libel Defense Resource Center, New York
Legal and Business Aspects of the Advertising Industry 1984, Practising Law Institute, New York
Legal and Business Aspects of the Magazine Industry, 1984, Practising Law Institute, New York
Libel Litigation, 1988 Practising Law Institute, New York
The Libel Revolution: A New Look at Defamation and Privacy, 1987, Law Arts Publishers, New York
Library and Classroom Use of Copyrighted Videotapes and Computer Software, American Library Association, Chicago, Illinois
Lindey on Entertainment, Publishing and the Arts, Agreements and the Law, Clark Boardman Company Ltd., New York
Making It Legal: A Law Primer for the Craftworker, Visual Artist & Writer, McGraw-Hill, New York
Making It Legal: A Legal Primer for Authors, Artists and Craftspeople, Northland Publishing, Flagstaff, Arizona
Martindale-Hubbell Legal Directory, Summit, New Jersey
Mass Media and the First Amendment, Wm. C. Brown Co., Dubuque, Iowa
Mass Media Law and Regulation, 1986, Wiley, New York
Media Law, 1987, Random House, New York
Media Law Dictionary, The, 1978, University Press of America, Washington, D.C.
Modern Intellectual Property, Prentice Hall Law and Business, Clifton, New Jersey
Paralegal Practice and Procedure, a Practical Guide for the Legal Assistant, 1986, Prentice Hall, Englewood Cliffs, New Jersey
Performing Arts Management & Law, 9 vols., Law Arts Publishers, New York
Photojournalism: The Professionals' Approach, 1980, Curtin and London, Somerville, Massachusetts
The Plain Language Law Dictionary, Penguin, New York
The Publishing Law Handbook, Prentice Hall Law and Business, Clifton, New Jersey
Reporter and the Law, The, Hastings House, New York
Reporter and the Law, The, American Newspaper Publishers Association Foundation, Washington, D.C.
Shepard's Acts and Cases by Popular Names, Federal and State, McGraw-Hill, New York
Summary of American Law, 1974, Lawyers Co-operative Publishing, Rochester
Trademark Law: A Practitioner's Guide, Practising Law Institute, New York
United States Code Service, Lawyers Co-operative Publishing, Rochester

Periodicals, Pamphlets & Looseleaf Services

American Lawyer, The, New York
The Annual Ethics Report, Society of Professional Journalists, Chicago

Case and Comment, Rochester

Celebrities and Privacy, Privacy Journal, Washington, D.C.

A Citizen's Guide on How to Use the Freedom of Information Act and the Privacy Act in Requesting Government Documents, 1987, U.S. Government Printing Office, Washington, D.C.

COMM/ENT, Hastings Communications and Entertainment Law Journal, Hastings Law School, University of California, San Francisco

Communications Lawyer, American Bar Association, Chicago

Compilation of State and Federal Privacy Laws, Privacy Journal, Washington, D.C.

The Computer Lawyer, Prentice Hall Law & Business, Clifton, New Jersey

Copyright Primer for Film and Video, Northwest Media Project, Portland, Oregon

Copyright Law Reporter, Commerce Clearing House, Inc., Chicago

Copyright: Staying Within the Law; A Resource Guide for Educators, PBS, Alexandria, Virginia

Entertainment Law Reporter, Santa Monica, California

Entertainment and Sports Lawyer, American Bar Association, Chicago

Everyday Law, Washington, D.C.

The First Amendment Handbook, Reporters Committee for Freedom of the Press, Washington, D.C.

Free Press/Fair Trial, American Newspaper Publishers Association Foundation, Washington, D.C.

Freedom of Information Report, Chicago, Illinois

How to Use the Federal Freedom of Information Act, Reporters Committee for Freedom of the Press, Washington, D.C.

LDRC Bulletin, Libel Defense Resource Center, New York

Legal Times, Washington, D.C.

Librarian's Guide to the New Copyright Law, American Library Association, Chicago

Loyola Entertainment Law Journal, Los Angeles, California

Media Law Reporter, Bureau of National Affairs, Inc., Washington, D.C.

National Law Journal, New York

News/Media and the Law, Reporters Committee for Freedom of the Press, Washington, D.C.

Photocopying by Academic, Public and Nonprofit Research Libraries, Association of American Publishers, Washington, D.C.

Practical Lawyer, The, Philadelphia

The Practical Tax Lawyer, Philadelphia, Pennsylvania

Preview of U.S. Supreme Court Cases, American Bar Association, Chicago

Privacy Journal, Washington, D.C.

School Law Bulletin, Chapel Hill, North Carolina

Synopsis of the Law of Libel and the Right of Privacy, World Almanac Publications, New York

Trial, Washington, D.C.

A Writer's Guide to Copyright, Poets and Writers, Inc., New York

A Writer's Guide to Ethical and Economic Issues, 1985 ASJA, New York

For additional new books as they are published, see a directory called *Subject Guide to Books in Print* at the public Library. Titles of interest will be found under the subject categories of:

Advertising Laws
Authors and Publishers
Journalism, Legal
Journalistic Ethics
Law—Bibliography
Law—Popular Works
Obscenity (Law)
Photography—Law and Legislation
Taxation—Law

Index

Actual injury, libel and, 4
Actual malice, proving, 3-4, 40
Ads, using names in, 16-17
Advance, 86
Agent
    difficulty of getting, 81
    as protection for writer, 81
    rights retained by, 96
Agreement, limiting term of
    syndicate, 110
"Alleged," used as protection, 31
*Anderson v. Avco Embassy Picures
    et al.*, 40
Appeals, on Social Security
    decisions, 135
Approved Production Contract for
    Dramatic Works, 103
Approved Production Contract for
    Musicals, 103
Ariel Sharon v. Time Magazine,
    32-33
Authors Guild, 92
Automatic renewal, avoiding, 110

Believability factor, in libel suits, 39-
    40
Benefits, for family members, 129
Bindrim v. Mitchell, 35-36
Book club
    licensing rights to, 88
    sales, 98-99
Book contract
    and copyright, 67-68
    obtaining sample of, 92
    subsidiary rights in, 87-89
    writer's vulnerability with first, 85
*Booth v. Curtis Publishing
    Company*, 16-17
British rights, 88

Canadian copyright, 69
Canons of Judicial Ethics, 54-55
*Cantrell v. Forest City Publishing
    Co.*, 18-19
Car expense, 116-117
Characters, disguising, 37-38
*Cher v. Forum International,
    Ltd.*, 17

Child pornography, 45-46
Clauses
    exclusivity, 110
    option, 90-91
    ownership and in perpetuity, 111
    warranty, 90
Commercial rights, 99
Community standards, of obscenity,
    43-44
Compensatory damages, 28
Composographs, 50
Contract
    book, 67-68, 85, 87-89, 92
    for dramatic works, 103
    five and five, 110
    movie and television, 103-107
    for musicals, 103
    syndication, 109-112
    ten and ten, 110
Copyright
    and contribution to magazine,
        62-63
    defined, 59-60
    duration of, 69-70
    and edited manuscript, 68
    of humor collection, 68
    and photographs, 51-52
    renewal by executor, 141
    signing away or keeping, 67
    and "substantially similar" work,
        76-78
    vs. rights, 68
Copyright guidelines, 64-65
Copyright law, for television and
    movie properties, 75-76
Copyright notice, omission of, 67
Copyright Office
    establishing date of creation
        through, 82
    registering with, 63, 67
Copyrighted material, fair use of, 64,
    71
Copyrighting unpublished material,
    61
Correction, as partial defense against
    libel, 31
Cox Broadcasting v. Cohn, 20-21
Creative control, maintaining, 110

Credits, getting tax, 125-127

Damages, as triple threat to
    publisher, 28-29
Date of creation, establishing, 81-83
Deductions
    allowed, 116-117
    for computer, 115
    for working at home, 113-114
    See also Tax, Home office
Defamation, 24
Depreciation
    car, write-offs for business, 117
    for office equipment, 115-116
Dialogue, reconstructed, 19
Disability
    insurance for, 129-133
    returning to work after, 132-133
Disclaimers, 37
Disclosure
    of distant pasts, 21-22
    of newsworthy facts, 19-20
Disguising characters, 37-38
Docudrama, and reconstructed
    dialogue, 19
Dramatists Guild, 103

Edited manuscript, and copyright,
    68
Editor vs.writer, as final guard
    against libel, 30-31
Endorsement, implied, 17
Equipment, deductions for, 115
Estate
        naming executor for, 139-140
    net, 143
    unpublished works as part of, 141-
    142
    using works belonging to, 143-144
Ethics, in photography, 55-57
Executor
    of author's estate, 139-140
    responsibilities of, 140-143
Exemptions, from clearance and
    royalty provisions, 71-72
Expenses
    car, 116-117
    writing off, 115

Fair comment, criteria for, 28
Fair use, of copyrighted material, 64,
    71

False light, 17-19
False pretenses, gathering news
    under, 14-15
Family members
    and disability insurance, 131-132
    Social Security benefits for, 129
Ferber v. New York, 45
Fiction
    libelous, 31
    plaintiff's responsibility to prove
        identification in, 36
    and public figures, 40-41
Fictionalization, of real-life events,
    17-19
First Amendment
    and freelance writers, 1-2
    and mass media, 9-10
    and student press, 10
First North American Serial Rights,
    66
First serial sales, decrease of, 97
Floater policy, 52
Foreign rights, 99
Free press, vs. fair trial, 8
Freedom of Information Act, 7-8
Freelance writers
    and libel, 2-5
    and shield law, 5-7
    vs. staff writers, 1-2

General interest exception, 16

Hawkins v. Multimedia, 21-22
*Hazelwood School District v.
    Kuhlmeier*, 10
Headlines, libelous, 30
Herbert v. Lando, 4
Hicks v. Casablanca Records, 40
Home office, limit on deductions for,
    114
Hospital insurance, 133-134
Humor collection, copyrighting, 68
Hustler Magazine v. Falwell, 3

Ideas, as ineligible for copyright,
    61, 76-78
Identification, and libel, 24
In camera, defined, 8
In perpetuity clauses, avoiding, 111
Independent Literary Agents
    Association, 92
Insurance

disability, 129-133
hospital, 133-134
  libel, 29-30
  medical, 134
  for photographers, 52-54
  survivors', 134-135
Intrusion, 14-15
Invasion of privacy, 5

Joint work, defined, 63
Journalists, vs. freelance writers,
  5-6

Kaplan v. California, 45

Legitimate public interest,
  defined, 4
Libel, 2-5
  and believability factor, 39-40
  and fiction, 31
  and photographs, 30-31, 50
  three elements of, 24
Libel insurance. *See* Insurance
Libel laws
  for magazines vs. newspapers, 29
  state-to-state differences in, 23
Libel suits, as political forum, 32-33
Libelous captions, 50
*Librarians Guide to the New
  Copyright Law*, 64
Life plus fifty term, 63
Literary adviser, for author's estate,
  140
Literary property, 74
Literature, serious, and
  obscenity, 44

Magazines, and libel laws, 29
Malice
  defined, 27-28
  public officials must prove, 26-27
Mass market paperbacks, 87-88
Mass market reprint rights, 89
Mass media, and the First
  Amendment, 9-10
Medical insurance, 134
Medicare, 133-134
Melvin v. Reid, 21
Miller v. California, 9, 43
Misappropriation, defined, 15-17
Misappropriation rules, exceptions

  to
general interest, 16
news, 15-16
Mishkin v. New York, 44
Model release
  obtaining written, 47-48
  sample, 49
Modified Accelerated Cost Recovery
  System, 114
Movie ideas, coincidental similarities
  in, 74-75
Movie rights
  as expanding market, 97-98
  See also Television

Namath v. Time Inc., 17
Net estate, defined, 143
Net income
  defined, 122
  limitations of, 114
Net receipts, royalties on, 87
New York Times rule, 26-27
New York Times v. Sullivan, 2-3
News exception, and right of privacy,
  15-16
News gathering, under false
  pretenses, 14-15
Newsworthiness factor, 4-5
Novelty, as factor in protecting
  properties, 79-80

Obscenity
  criteria for defining, 43
  and photographs; 51
  problems in defining, 8-9
  and serious literary works, 44
Option clause, 90-91
Optional method, of reporting
  income, 122-125
Ownership clauses, avoiding, 111

Paperback reprints, 96-97
Paperback rights, 87-88
Partial retirement, 128-129
Patently offensive, 43-44
Payment
  to author from publisher, 91
  for photographic services, 57
  See also Advance, Royalties
Permission
  from photographic subject, 47-48

using photographs without, 15-17
for using works belonging to estate,
 143-144
*Photocopying by Academic, Public
 and Non-profit Research
 Libraries*, 64
Photographic services, pricing, 57
Photographic subject, getting
 permission from, 47-48
Photographs
 copyrighting, 51-52
 dealing with authorities to obtain,
 54-55
 and good taste, 56-57
 libelous, 30-31, 50
 obscene, 50
 used without permission, 15-17
Photography, ethics in, 55-57
Photography business, running, 55
Pinkus v. United States, 43
Playwrights, 103
Pornography. *See* Obscenity
Pretrial publicity, 55
Preventive journalism, 24-25
Pring v. Penthouse, 39
Prior restraint, 1-2
Producer
 letter from, for unsolicited
 material, 82-83
 option of, to refuse disclosure,
 80-81
Properties
 deciding when to sell, 98
 non-copyright protection for,
 78-81
Protecting ideas, for movies and
 television, 74-75
Prurient interest, 44
Public broadcasting, and copyrighted
 materials, 70-71
Public disclosure privacy, 19-22
Public interest, and malice, 27
Public records, using facts from,
 20-21
Public Telecommunications Review,
 64
Public's right to know vs. subject's
 right to privacy, 13
Publication
 and libel, 24
 of old letters, 70
 and public domain, 70

without notice of copyright, 61-62
Publisher's obligations, 91-92
Publisher's rights, 89-90, 96
Publishing, once-and-done, 116
Punitive damages, 28-29

Quarterly payments, 125-127
Questions to ask, to avoid libel, 32
Quoting, from copyrighted material,
 66-67

Receipts, importance of keeping, 116
Record keeping, 116
Rejection slips, as evidence of
 working, 118
Renaming characters, in fiction, 37
Renewing copyrights, as executor's
 responsibility, 141
Reporting, balanced and accurate, 26
Reprint rights
 mass market, 89
 selling, 66
Reprinters, increased caution on part
 of, 97
Retirement benefits, for self-
 employed writers, 127-129
Revised copyright law, 60-61
Right of privacy
 defined, 13-14
 and photographic subject, 48-49
Rights
 British, 88
 commercial, 99
 foreign, 99
 movie, 88, 97-98
 paperback, 87-88
 publisher's, 89-90, 96
 reprint, 89
 retained by agent, 96
 subsidiary, 87-88
 translation, 88, 99-100
 vs. copyright, 68
Rights infringement, 68-69
Royalties
 book club, 98-99
 received through trust funds, 142-
 143
 standard, 86-87

Safe harbor three year rule, 115
Self-employment tax, 125
Shield law, 5-7

Sidis v. F-R Publishing Corp, 21
Signed statement, for disclosing
    unsolicited material, 82-83
Single publication rule, 24
Social Security, qualifying for,
    121-125
Social Security benefits
  for family members, 129
  for retirees, 127-129
Social Security decisions, appealing,
    135
Social Security tax, 117
Society of Authors' Representatives,
    92
Softcover book. *See* Paperback
Spahn v. Julian Messner, Inc., 18
Special damages, 28
Springer v. Viking Press, 38-39
SSI. *See* Supplemental Security
    Income
Straight line method, of calculating
    depreciation, 114
Student press, and the First
    Amendment, 10
Subsidiary rights, in book contract,
    87-88
Supplemental Security Income, 135-
    137
Survivors' insurance, 134-135
Syndicate agreement
  standard, 111
  suggestions for negotiating,
    109-112
Synopses, for movie rights, 98

Taping phone calls, 15
Tax
  self-employment, 125
  Social Security, 117
Tax credits, 125-127
Tax forms, 117-118
Tax payments, estimated, 117
Tax policies, state-to-state
    differences in, 143

Television
  movies made for, 97-98
  See also Properties
Television and motion piciture
    rights, 88
Television compensation, WGA
    agreement for, 105-107
Theatrical compensation, WGA
    agreement for, 104
Time Inc. v. Firestone, 27
Time Inc. v. Hill, 18, 27
Times v. Sullivan, 27
*Tinker v. Des Moines Independent
    School District*, 10
Titles, protection of, 69
Topping privileges, 110
Trade paperbacks, 87-88
Transfer of copyright, 63
Translation rights
  as expanding market, 99-100
  publisher's percentage of, 88
Trust funds, 142-143
Truth, as defense against libel,
    25-26

Unpublished works, as executor's
    responsibility, 141-142
Unsolicited material, signing
    statement to submit, 82-83

Virgil v. Time Inc., 19-20

Warranty clause, 90
Wheeler v. Dell Publishing Co., 38
Will. *See* Estate, Executor
Wiretapping, 15
Writer's Market, 92
Writers
  and the First Amendment, 1-2
  resources for, 92
Writers Guild of America
    Registration Service, 82

Zurcher v. Stanford Daily, 2

Other Books of Interest

Annual Market Books

Artist's Market, edited by Susan Conner $19.95
Children's Writer's & Illustrator's Market, edited by Connie Eidenier (paper) $14.95
Novel & Short Story Writer's Market, edited by Laurie Henry (paper) $17.95
Photographer's Market, edited by Sam Marshall $19.95
Poet's Market, by Judson Jerome $18.95
Songwriter's Market, edited by Mark Garvey $18.95
Writer's Market, edited by Glenda Neff $23.95

General Writing Books

Annable's Treasury of Literary Teasers, by H.D. Annable (paper) $10.95
Beginning Writer's Answer Book, edited by Kirk Polking (paper) $12.95
Beyond Style: Mastering the Finer Points of Writing, by Gary Provost $15.95
Discovering the Writer Within, by Bruce Ballenger & Barry Lane $16.95
Getting the Words Right: How to Revise, Edit and Rewrite, by Theodore A. Rees Cheney $15.95
A Handbook of Problem Words & Phrases, by Morton S. Freeman $16.95
How to Increase Your Word Power, by the editors of Reader's Digest $19.95
How to Write a Book Proposal, by Michael Larsen $10.95
Just Open a Vein, edited by William Brohaugh $15.95
Knowing Where to Look: The Ultimate Guide to Research, by Lois Horowitz (paper) $15.95
Make Every Word Count, by Gary Provost (paper) $9.95
On Being a Writer, edited by Bill Strickland $19.95
Pinckert's Practical Grammar, by Robert C. Pinckert $14.95
The Story Behind the Word, by Morton S. Freeman (paper) $9.95
12 Keys to Writing Books that Sell, by Kathleen Krull (paper) $12.95
The 29 Most Common Writing Mistakes & How to Avoid Them, by Judy Delton $9.95
Word Processing Secrets for Writers, by Michael A. Banks & Ansen Dibell (paper) $14.95
Writer's Block & How to Use It, by Victoria Nelson $14.95
The Writer's Digest Guide to Manuscript Formats, by Buchman & Groves $16.95
Writer's Encyclopedia, edited by Kirk Polking (paper) $16.95

Nonfiction Writing

Basic Magazine Writing, by Barbara Kevles $16.95
How to Sell Every Magazine Article You Write, by Lisa Collier Cool (paper) $11.95
The Writer's Digest Handbook of Magazine Article Writing, edited by Jean M. Fredette $15.95
Writing Creative Nonfiction, by Theodore A. Rees Cheney $15.95
Writing Nonfiction that Sells, by Samm Sinclair Baker $14.95

Fiction Writing

The Art & Craft of Novel Writing, by Oakley Hall $16.95
Best Stories from New Writers, edited by Linda Sanders $16.95
Characters & Viewpoint, by Orson Scott Card $13.95
Creating Short Fiction, by Damon Knight (paper) $9.95
Dare to Be a Great Writer: 329 Keys to Powerful Fiction, by Leonard Bishop $15.95
Dialogue, by Lewis Turco $12.95
Fiction is Folks: How to Create Unforgettable Characters, by Robert Newton Peck (paper) $8.95
Handbook of Short Story Writing: Vol. I, by Dickson and Smythe (paper) $9.95
Handbook of Short Story Writing: Vol. II, edited by Jean M. Fredette $15.95
One Great Way to Write Short Stories, by Ben Nyberg $14.95
Plot, by Ansen Dibell $13.95
Revision, by Kit Reed $13.95
Spider Spin Me a Web: Lawrence Block on Writing Fiction, by Lawrence Block $16.95
Storycrafting, by Paul Darcy Boles (paper) $10.95
Writing the Novel: From Plot to Print, by Lawrence Block (paper) $9.95

Special Interest Writing Books

The Children's Picture Book: How to Write It, How to Sell It, by Ellen E.M. Roberts (paper) $16.95

Comedy Writing Secrets, by Melvin Helitzer $18.95
The Complete Book of Scriptwriting, by J. Michael Straczynski (paper) $11.95
The Craft of Lyric Writing, by Sheila Davis $18.95
Editing Your Newsletter, by Mark Beach (paper) $18.50
Families Writing, by Peter Stillman $15.95
Guide to Greeting Card Writing, edited by Larry Sandman (paper) $9.95
How to Write a Play, by Raymond Hull (paper) $12.95
How to Write Action/Adventure Novels, by Michael Newton $13.95
How to Write & Sell A Column, by Raskin & Males $10.95
How to Write and Sell Your Personal Experiences, by Lois Duncan (paper) $10.95
How to Write Mysteries, by Shannon OCork $13.95
How to Write Romances, by Phyllis Taylor Pianka $13.95
How to Write Tales of Horror, Fantasy & Science Fiction, edited by J.N. Williamson $15.95
How to Write the Story of Your Life, by Frank P. Thomas (paper) $11.95
How to Write Western Novels, by Matt Braun $13.95
Mystery Writer's Handbook, by The Mystery Writers of America (paper) $10.95
The Poet's Handbook, by Judson Jerome (paper) $10.95
Successful Lyric Writing (workbook), by Sheila Davis (paper) $16.95
Successful Scriptwriting, by Jurgen Wolff & Kerry Cox $18.95
Travel Writer's Handbook, by Louise Zobel (paper) $11.95
TV Scriptwriter's Handbook, by Alfred Brenner (paper) $10.95
Writing for Children & Teenagers, 3rd Edition, by Lee Wyndham & Arnold Madison (paper) $12.95
Writing Short Stories for Young People, by George Edward Stanley $15.95
Writing the Modern Mystery, by Barbara Norville $15.95
Writing to Inspire, edited by William Gentz (paper) $14.95

The Writing Business
A Beginner's Guide to Getting Published, edited by Kirk Polking $11.95
The Complete Guide to Self-Publishing, by Tom & Marilyn Ross (paper) $16.95
How to Sell & Re-Sell Your Writing, by Duane Newcomb $11.95
How to Write with a Collaborator, by Hal Bennett with Michael Larsen $11.95
Is There a Speech Inside You?, by Don Aslett (paper) $9.95
Literary Agents: How to Get & Work with the Right One for You, by Michael Larsen $9.95
Professional Etiquette for Writers, by William Brohaugh $9.95
Time Management for Writers, by Ted Schwarz $10.95
The Writer's Friendly Legal Guide, edited by Kirk Polking $16.95
A Writer's Guide to Contract Negotiations, by Richard Balkin (paper) $11.95

To order directly from the publisher, include $3.00 postage and handling for 1 book and 50¢ for each additional book. Allow 30 days for delivery.

Writer's Digest Books
1507 Dana Avenue, Cincinnati, Ohio 45207
Credit card orders call TOLL-FREE
1-800-543-4644 (Outside Ohio)
1-800-551-0884 (Ohio only)
Prices subject to change without notice.

Write to this same address for information on *Writer's Digest* magazine, Writer's Digest Book Club, Writer's Digest School, and Writer's Digest Criticism Service.